India-UK Collaborations and Investments in Food Supply Chain

ABOUT THE AUTHORS:

Dipankar De is a Partner at D&B Tangram Advisory Services Pvt. Ltd. He has worked with several central and state government organisations in India, including Ministry of Textiles, Ministry of Science and Technology, Ministry of Food Processing Industries, Small Industries Development Bank of India (SIDBI) and multilateral organisations such as Gesellschaft für Internationale Zusammenarbeit (GIZ), KfW Development Bank, Japan External Trade Organization (JETRO). He has worked with a number of global and Indian corporate on business development and go-to-market strategies; and has also worked across various sectors, including food and agri-business, healthcare, cement, automotive, etc. He is an MPhil in Economics from the Calcutta University and an MBA from XLRI Jamshedpur.

Arpita Mukherjee is a Professor at Indian Council for Research on International Economic Relations (ICRIER). She has several years of experience in policy-oriented research, working closely with the government in India and policymakers in the EU, US, ASEAN and in East Asian countries. She has conducted studies for international organisations and Indian industry associations. She has authored chapters in joint study group reports set up by Indian government and has led research teams contributing to India's domestic policy reforms in areas such as logistics, retail, special economic zones and mega food parks. Dr Mukherjee has a PhD in Economics from the University of Portsmouth, UK. She has published widely and presented her research in various international and national forums.

Nikhil Khurana is a Senior Consultant at D&B Tangram Advisory Services Pvt. Ltd. He has executed multiple assignments for various corporate clients, government ministries and institutions and multilateral organisations. He has extensive experience in the area of market entry and opportunity assessment, industry analysis and research, business planning, etc. across various sectors, including food and agri-business, IT and ITES, logistics & supply chain, BFSI. He specialises in conducting qualitative and quantitative research and analysis. He holds a Masters degree in Business Administration with specialisation in Marketing and International Business, from IMSAR, MDU University, Haryana.

Tanu M. Goyal is a Consultant at ICRIER. Her research interests include trade in services, retail sector, food supply chain, international trade agreements and policy and regulatory issues. Most of her work concerns trade, openness and restructuring of the Indian economy in the global landscape. At ICRIER, Tanu has worked on several projects for the Indian government, international aid agencies such as the Asian Development Bank (ADB), European Commission (EC) and academic institutions such as the Indian Institute of Management (IIM). She has published several international and national journal articles, book chapters, reports and other popular media articles on policy issues. She holds a Masters degree in Economics with specialisation in world economy, from Centre of Trade and Development (CITD), Jawaharlal Nehru University, New Delhi.

Bhavook Bhardwaj is a Research Assistant at ICRIER. His research interests include international trade and trade in services. At ICRIER, he has worked on projects for the Indian government and international agencies such as the European Commission; and has contributed to policy reports and has also contributed to the Working Paper Series. He has a Masters degree in Economics with specialisation in environment and resource economics from TERI University, New Delhi.

Rohini Sanyal was an Associate Consultant with D&B Tangram Advisory Services Pvt Ltd. She has worked on projects with GIZ, KfW Development Bank on studies involving industry research, financial & economic policies and market entry strategy. She has completed her Master's degree in Economics from the University of Warwick, UK. She is currently working as an Associate in Bain & Company.

India-UK Collaborations and Investments in Food Supply Chain

Opportunities, Concerns and the Way Forward

ACADEMIC FOUNDATION
NEW DELHI

www.academicfoundation.org

First published in 2016
by

ACADEMIC FOUNDATION
4772-73 / 23 Bharat Ram Road, (23 Ansari Road),
Darya Ganj, New Delhi - 110 002 (India).
Phones : 23245001 / 02 / 03 / 04.
Fax : +91-11-23245005.
E-mail : books@academicfoundation.com
www.academicfoundation.com

and

DUN & BRADSTREET TANGRAM ADVISORY SERVICES PVT LTD
Indiabulls Finance Centre, Tower Two, 14th Floor,
Senapati Bapat Marg, Elphinstone Road (W), Mumbai - 400013.
Phone: T: 91 22 4922 1000/ 1006
Fax: 91 22 4922 1010
Email: admin@dnbtangram.com
www.dnbtangram.com ; www.foodlogistics.in

India-UK Collaborations and Investments in Food Supply Chain: Opportunities, Concerns and the Way Forward

by Dipankar De, Arpita Mukherjee, Nikhil Khurana, Tanu M. Goyal, Bhavook Bhardwaj and Rohini Sanyal

ISBN 9789332703636

Typeset, printed and bound by The Book Mint, New Delhi.
www.thebookmint.in

Contents

List of Tables, Figures and Boxes

Tables

Figures

Boxes

Foreword

The logistics and supply chain performance is currently impacting India's global competitiveness by increasing operating costs and capital expenditures, delays and unpredictability, reduction in overall business activities and restricting potential integration with global value chains. It is well-known that India's logistics cost at present is as high as 13-14 per cent of the gross domestic product (GDP).

A typical case in point is the food supply chain in India where there are substantial wastages across various stages in the supply chain. Critical logistical infrastructural gaps, essential skill gaps across functions and inadequate research and development (R&D) in the food supply chain are a few of the specific immediate areas of attention. Improving efficiency and unlocking potential in the food supply chain, therefore, has been a key priority for the current government who is actively encouraging foreign investments in supply chain sectors such as storage and warehousing, cold-chain, packaging, skill development and R&D.

The Indian Prime Minister Shri Narendra Damodardas Modi's visit to the United Kingdom (UK) in November 2015 has facilitated several collaborations, partnerships and knowledge sharing between India and the UK. The Government of India's initiatives such as 'Make in India' and 'Start-up India' coupled with high growth rate of the country, a large growing middle class and the growth of organised retail have made the Indian market more accessible and attractive for the UK companies. Alongside, the UK government has strong focus on food and drink sector and its exports. With their advanced supply chain management practices, the UK companies can help reduce wastages in the supply chain and increase the shelf life of products. The UK and EU markets are getting saturated and India is a fast growing market. Investment in this market will help the UK companies increase their global presence. All these factors can lead to more investment flows from the UK and collaborations in the food supply chain, which are mutually beneficial.

Against this background, the objective of this study is to examine the scope for improving the efficiency of the food supply chain in India through collaborations and investment inflows from the UK. The study focuses on five areas of the food supply chain, namely storage and warehousing, cold-chains, packaging technology, skill development and R&D. It provides an overview of each of these segments in India and the UK, examines the regulations, identifies the areas of collaborations and examines the barriers faced by the UK companies in India. It then makes policy recommendations and suggests a go-to-market strategy for the UK companies.

To understand the present operating environment and the scope for future investments and foreign collaborations in each of the five segments, D&B Tangram Advisory Services Pvt Ltd (D&B Tangram) has undertaken consultations with multiple stakeholders during the course of the study including several policy makers in India and the UK, sector experts, Indian and the UK companies, association and industry bodies among others. In addition, an advisory committee was set up and their inputs were sought during course of the project.

The report provides a unique understanding of what impinges the efficiency across various sub-sectors in the food supply chain. While some issues are general, others are sector specific. Some barriers are obstructing the entry of the UK businesses in India, while others offer an opportunity to foreign businesses to invest in the Indian market.

This study recommends measures for improving efficiency and investments through multitude of actions from various stakeholders including the government, regulatory bodies, industry associations and businesses. Greater coordination and collaboration among these bodies will enhance the overall competitiveness of the sector. Hastening of various policy and regulatory reforms like land acquisition, foreign direct investment (FDI) in multi-brand retail, implementation of Goods and Services Tax (GST) are likely to improve the business conditions. Implementation of 'green channelling' for agri-produce to reduce wastage, increasing centre-state coordination to improve investor confidence, bringing in more transparency and awareness about government policies, simplifying customs procedures and food safety regulations are other key recommendations.

A change in approach from warehouse creation to warehouse management including bringing in better technology, increasing throughputs is recommended. The report suggests encouraging investment in weak links in the cold-chain infrastructure of reefer vehicles and pack-houses and taking an integrated approach towards developing a cold-chain grid in the country. Further, lowering of taxes on processed food and incentivising R&D and innovation in specific areas will encourage investment and collaborations in the packaging technology sector. With changes in consumer behaviour and food habits impacting food logistics, the approach to skill development towards vocational training needs changes to address the emerging skill gaps. Collaborative effort from the government and corporates to establish joint skill development centres, developing short-term online courses in warehousing, cold-chain and packaging technology, promoting on-the-job training and training of trainers are recommended to unlock potential in the skill development sector. Businesses should be given incentives for undertaking R&D in sectors such as food processing and food supply chain and these should be made priority sectors for encouraging R&D and innovation under the 'Start-up India' initiative.

The report charts out clear action points for UK Trade & Investment (UKTI) in India and UK India Business Council (UKIBC) to increase awareness and market understanding of the UK companies and work collaboratively with the centre and state governments in India to enhance India-UK trade and investment in food supply chain. This will lead to benefits for both Indian and the UK companies.

This report is a culmination of extensive research during the year-long project and provides a wealth of information on the broad topic of food supply chain. The findings of the report will be a useful repository of knowledge and provide action agenda in the short- to medium-term for policy makers, government, regulators, industry and academia. The study will benefit the policy makers and regulators of both the countries to address the much needed reforms to boost the growth and development of the food supply chain and logistics. I am sure that the findings of the report will enhance market understanding of the UK companies in the five key areas of their interest and help them formulate the go-to-market strategies for the Indian market.

The current project funded by the Foreign and Commonwealth Office (FCO) of the British High Commission, UK, is amongst the series of work done in the food supply chain, which is one of the key focus areas of research at D&B Tangram. I am sure that the website developed under the project, *www.foodlogistics.in* will provide a good platform to exchange ideas, disseminate information about the Indian market to the UK companies across a wide range of areas in the food supply chain. D&B Tangram gratefully acknowledges support from the FCO, British High Commission.

—Priyaa Gurnani

Director

D&B Tangram Advisory Services Pvt Ltd

Acknowledgements

We would like to extend special thanks to all those who provided us support during the project, 'Enhancing India's Competitiveness through Logistics and Supply Chain Efficiency'. First of all, we would like to take this opportunity to thank the Foreign and Commonwealth Office (FCO) of the British High Commission, United Kingdom (UK) for sponsoring this study. We express our great appreciation to Mr Gaurav Gurung, Ms Yashodhara Dasgupta, and Ms Kiraan Sharma for their constant support and encouragement during the course of the project.

We especially thank several policy makers, senior government officials at central and state level, multiple government organisations, industry bodies and experts in India and the UK who enhanced our understanding of the subject. The authors have benefitted from discussions with Dr Jyoti Bhat and Dr Sanjeev K. Varshney, Adviser/Scientist "G", Department of Science and Technology, Government of India (GoI); Dr Shailja Gupta, Director, Department of Biotechnology, GoI; Dr S.K. Goel, Ex-Additional Chief Secretary, Agriculture and Marketing, Government of Maharashtra; Dr Maninder Kaur Dwivedi, Executive Director (Personnel), Food Corporation of India (FCI); Mr Harpreet Singh, Managing Director, Central Warehousing Corporation (CWC); Mr Pawanexh Kohli, Chief Executive Officer (CEO) and Chief Advisor, National Centre for Cold-chain Development (NCCD); Dr Sudhanshu, Deputy General Manager, Agricultural & Processed Food Products Export Development Authority (APEDA), Mumbai; Dr N.C. Saha, Director, Indian Institute of Packaging; Mr K. Narayan, Group General Manager (Strategic Planning), Container Corporation of India Limited (CONCOR); Dr Ashutosh Upadhyay, Dean (Academics), National Institute of Food Technology Entrepreneurship and Management; Mr Vimal Kumar, Deputy Director, Global Innovations & Technology Alliance (GITA); Mr B. Thiagarajan, Executive Director & President, Blue Star Limited; Mr Nitin Puri, Senior President and Country Head, Food & Agri Strategic Advisory & Research at Yes Bank.

We would like to thank Mr Tony Lamb from Department for Environment Food & Rural Affairs (DEFRA), UK Government; Mr Graham Nicholas from UK Trade & Investment (UKTI), UK Government; and Ms Tessa Kelly from British Retail Consortium (BRC), among others. We extend special thanks to Ms Tara Panjwani, UK India Business Council (UKIBC) for her assistance during the project for organising webinars, industry interactions and sharing useful insights on critical business expectations of the UK companies.

We would also like to thank all the distinguished members of the advisory committee for their constant support and guidance throughout the tenure of the project.

We would also like to thank all the Indian and foreign companies, retail and supply chain businesses and associations that have taken their valuable time out from their busy schedule and provided us with information and insights on their experiences, market dynamics, challenges faced and expectations.

We specially thank all the speakers, panelist and participants who had attended our seminar, 'Enhancing India's Competitiveness through Logistics and Supply Chain Efficiency' in Mumbai held on 28 October 2015. We would like to thank all the participants from various countries who have attended our webinars, 'Food Logistics and Supply Chain in India: Opportunities for Investments and Collaborations' and 'Insights into the Indian Retail, Food and Drink Policy Scenario' held on 19 August 2015 and 19 November 2015, respectively. We would also like to thank all the participants who attended the presentation in London on 23 February 2016 titled, 'Future of Retail Market in India' by Dr Aprita Mukherjee, Professor, Indian Council for Research on International Economic Relations (ICRIER).

This study draws some of the key inputs from our earlier joint study with ICRIER titled, 'Evaluation of the Impact of the Scheme for Mega Food Park of the Ministry of Food Processing Industries'. We would like to thank the Ministry of Food Processing Industries (MoFPI) and the survey participants of that project, especially the mega food park developers whose inputs on storage and warehousing, cold-chains and R&D have been summarised in this report. We express our sincere thanks to Ms Harsimrat Kaur Badal, Union Minister, Ministry of Food Processing Industries, GoI; Mr Siraj Hussain, Ex-Secretary, Department of Agriculture, Cooperation and Farmers Welfare, Ministry of Agriculture, GoI; and Mr J.P. Meena, Additional Secretary, Ministry of Food Processing Industries, GoI.

We would like to thank Ms Priyaa Gurnani, Director, Dun & Bradstreet Tangram Advisory Services Pvt Ltd for giving us all the support and encouragement to work during the project. Suyog Keluskar, Medha Chowdhry and Shilpi Majumdar deserve special thanks for contributing at different stages of this report. We would like to thank Swetapadma Mohanty and team for helping us in organising the report release.

We would like to thank Nandita Singha for copyediting the report and Sona Kapila and Sanu Kapila of Academic Foundation for responding positively to our last-minute request for publication.

Finally, we express our deepest gratitude to our families for their constant support while we handled late night work pressures to successfully complete all project deliverables.

Abbreviations

3PL	Third Party Logistics
4PL	Fourth Party Logistics
AMI	Agricultural Marketing Infrastructure
ASEAN	Association of Southeast Asian Nations
BIS	Bureau of Indian Standards
BRC	British Retail Consortium
BTIA	Broad-based Trade and Investment Agreement
CAGR	Compound Annual Growth Rate
CAP	Cover and Plinth
CFS	Container Freight Station
CII	Confederation of Indian Industry
CMSD	Centre for Market Research & Social Development
CONCOR	Container Corporation of India
CSR	Corporate Social Responsibility
CWC	Central Warehousing Corporation
DBT	Department of Biotechnology
DeitY	Department of Electronics and Information Technology
DFC	Dedicated Freight Corridor
DIPP	Department of Industrial Policy and Promotion
DMIC	Delhi Mumbai Industrial Corridor
DSIR	Department of Scientific and Industrial Research
DST	Department of Science and Technology
EU	European Union
FCI	Food Corporation of India
FCO	Foreign Commonwealth Office
FDI	Foreign Direct Investment
FICCI	Federation of Indian Chamber of Commerce and Industry
FIPB	Foreign Investment Promotion Board
FMCG	Fast Moving Consumer Goods
FP7	Seventh Framework Programme
FSA	Food Standards Agency
FSSAI	Food Safety and Standards Authority of India
FTA	Free Trade Agreement
FTWZ	Free Trade Warehousing Zone
FY	Financial Year
GBP	Great Britain Pound
GDP	Gross Domestic Product
GERD	Gross Expenditure on Research and Development
GIR	Geographical Indications Registered
GITA	Global Innovation and Technology Alliance
GoI	Government of India
GPS	Global Positioning System
GST	Goods and Services Tax
IARW	International Association of Refrigerated Warehouses
ICD	Inland Container Depot
ICT	Information and Communication Technology
IIMM	Indian Institute of Materials Management
IIP	Indian Institute of Packaging
IL&FS	Infrastructure Leasing & Financial Services
ILO	International Labour Organization
IMF	International Monetary Fund
ING	International Netherlands Group
INR	Indian National Rupee
IPR	Intellectual Property Rights
IQF	Individual Quick Freezing
ISO	International Organization for Standardization
IT	Information Technology
ITC	Industrial Training Centre
ITI	Industrial Training Institute
ITMMA	Institute of Transport and Maritime Management Antwerp
km	Kilometre
LARR	Land Acquisition, Rehabilitation and Resettlement
LNG	Liquefied Natural Gas
MFP	Mega Food Park
MHRD	Ministry of Human Resource Development
MITIs	Model Industrial Training Centres
MoCI	Ministry of Commerce and Industry
MoD	Ministry of Defence
MoFPI	Ministry of Food Processing Industries

MoHFW	Ministry of Health and Family Welfare
MoU	Memorandum of Understanding
MSDE	Ministry of Skill Development and Entrepreneurship
MSME	Micro, Small and Medium Enterprise
MT	Metric Tonne
NABARD	National Bank for Agriculture and Rural Development
NCCD	National Centre for Cold-chain Development
NGO	Non-governmental Organisation
NSDA	National Skill Development Agency
NSDC	National Skill Development Corporation
NSQF	National Skills Qualification Framework
NSS	National Sample Survey
PPP	Public-Private Partnership
QSR	Quick Service Restaurant
R&D	Research and Development
RBI	Reserve Bank of India
RFID	Radio Frequency Identification
RIDF	Rural Infrastructure Development Fund
RTITB	Road Transport Industry Training Board
SEZ	Special Economic Zone
SAARC	South Asian Association for Regional Cooperation
SLCM	Sohan Lal Commodities Management
SME	Small and Medium Enterprise
SRISHTI	Science, Research and Innovation System for High Technology-led Path for India
SSC	Sector Skill Council
SWC	State Warehousing Corporation
TRIPS	Trade-Related Aspects of Intellectual Property Rights
UK	United Kingdom
UKIBC	UK India Business Council
UKIERI	UK-India Education and Research Initiative
UKTI	UK Trade & Investment
UKWA	United Kingdom Warehousing Association
UNESCO	United Nations Educational, Scientific and Cultural Organization
US	United States
USD	United States Dollar
VAT	Value-added Tax
WDRA	Warehousing Development and Regulatory Authority
WIF	Warehousing Infrastructure Fund
WIPO	World Intellectual Property Organization
WTO	World Trade Organization

Introduction

> A logistics task is defined as the process of strategically managing the procurement, movement and storage of materials, parts and finished inventory (and the related information flows) through the organization and its marketing channels in such a way that current and future profitability are maximized through the cost effective fulfilment of orders (Christopher, 1998: 4, taken from Fernie and Sparks, 2004).

Logistics and supply chain efficiency are crucial to systematic and timely delivery of goods and services in any country. This efficiency may be in terms of faster delivery of goods or reduced cost of transportation. An efficient logistics and supply chain is more important in the case of food products as they are perishable in nature and require a temperature-controlled environment (Smith and Sparks, 2004). Unlike the developed countries, developing countries such as India face infrastructure bottlenecks, and fragmented supply chain with lack of modern storage and transportation facilities. India also has the challenge of feeding its large population base and, at the same time, increasing its share in global trade, especially exports. Only by enhancing its logistics and supply chain efficiencies, India can develop as a global agriculture and food processing hub.

It is now a well-established fact that India is one of the largest producers of a number of agricultural products in the world. The country ranks second in the production of fruits and vegetables in the world, after China. During 2013–14, India produced 88.98 million metric tonnes (MT) of fruits and 162.89 million MT of vegetables.[1] In the same period, the area under cultivation of fruits stood at 7.22 million hectares while vegetables were cultivated in 9.40 million hectares, which in aggregate is approximately 7 per cent of the total cropped area of the country.[2] India is also the largest producer of milk and is among the top global producers of meat and poultry products. Further, with a growing domestic population, India is one of the largest consumer bases of agricultural produce. However, a number of studies have shown that the actual availability of agricultural produce to Indian consumers is low due to huge wastages in the supply chain. For example, Chari and Raghavan (2012) and Parfitt et al. (2010) estimated the total wastage in agricultural produce to be around 25–30 per cent. In a report prepared for Ministry of Food Processing Industries (MoFPI) in 2014, Yes Bank estimated the annual loss of fruits and vegetables at 18 per cent, pulses and cereals at 6 per cent, fish at 5.3 per cent, poultry at 3.7 per cent, meat at 2.3 per cent and milk at 0.8 per cent.[3]

Before one examines the causes for wastage in the supply chain, it is important to understand the food supply chain in India. From the point of production to consumption, there are several stages involved in the food supply chain (see Figure 1.0). These include storage and warehousing, and cold-chain and packaging, among others. At present, in India the infrastructure in each of these categories is either lacking, or not up to the global standards, which leads to wastages.

The National Centre for Cold-chain Development (NCCD) 2015 data shows that there is a huge demand-supply gap in logistics infrastructure. There is a need for pack-houses and ripening chambers, storage (temperature-controlled and ambient) and warehouses, processing units and reefer vehicles to transport the products at each stage. The study further highlights that the establishment of cold-chain infrastructure has been non-uniform across the states, with Uttar Pradesh, West Bengal and Gujarat having substantial storage capacities, while the north-eastern states of Sikkim, Manipur and Mizoram have very low storage capacities. There are hardly any storage facilities at the *mandis*[4] and there is significant shortage of pack-houses and refrigerated vehicles. A large country like India has only 249 pack-houses and most of them are used for exports. Thus, there are gaps in the logistics infrastructure, which leads to wastage.

Further, existing studies [for example, see KPMG (2007), National Skill Development Corporation (NSDC) (2009) and Kushwaha and Nath (2015)] have shown that there is a need for developing skills in specific segments of food supply chain to operate sophisticated machinery and infrastructure. Skilled workforce will help to reduce the wastages due to mishandling. There is also a need for research and development (R&D) in specific sectors of food supply chain that requires technology transfer and investments from others countries. R&D can help supply chain to not only modernise but also reduce wastages. Packaging technology can help increase the shelf life of produce and reduce wastages. It also helps to reduce the transportation costs.

1. National Horticulture Board, Government of India. Available at: *http://www.nhb.gov.in/area-pro/NHB_Database_2015.pdf* (accessed on 30 November 2015).
2. Department of Scientific and Industrial Research, Ministry of Science and Technology, Government of India. Available at: *http://dsir.gov.in/reports/ittp_tedo/agro/AF_Farm_Fruits_Vegetables_Intro.pdf* (accessed on 30 November 2015).
3. For details see Ministry of Food Processing Industries (MoFPI) and Yes Bank (2014)
4. A *mandi* is a market for selling fruits and vegetables and other agricultural commodities.

Figure 1.0

A Typical Supply Chain of Fruits and Vegetables in India

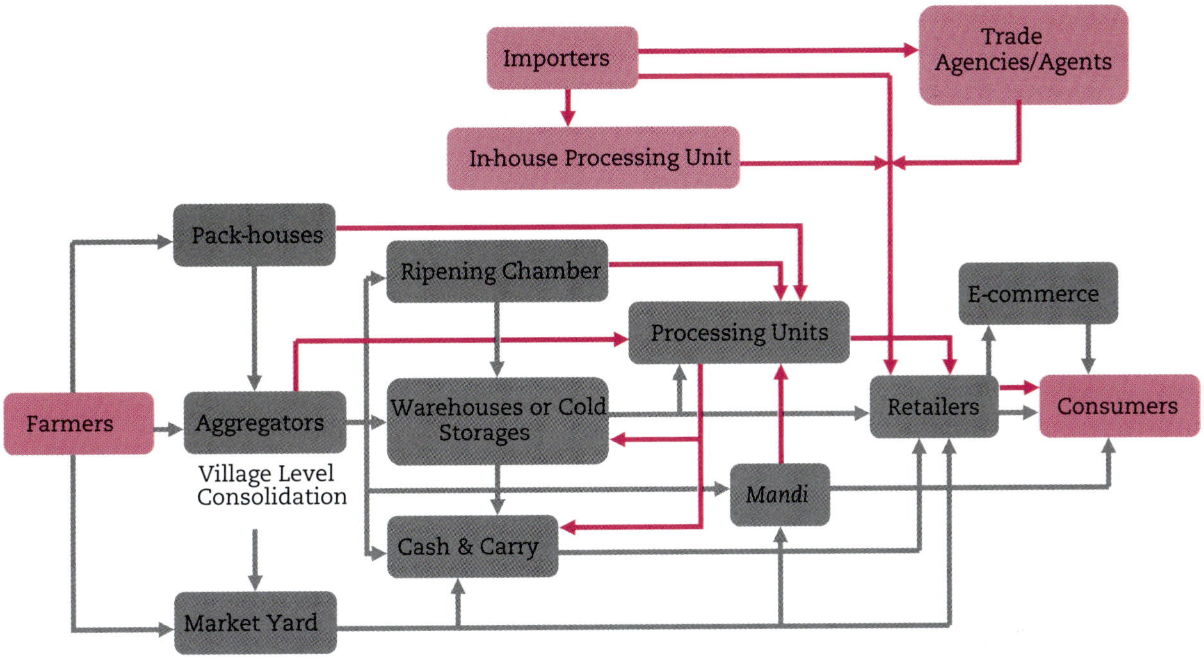

Source: Authors' discussion with supply chain agents.

Recognising the need to improve efficiency in the food supply chain, food logistics has been identified as a priority sector in India for foreign collaborations and investments. The government is actively encouraging foreign investors to invest in sectors such as storage and warehousing, cold-chain, packaging, skill development and R&D in food supply chain.

In November 2015, the government initiated a series of foreign direct investment (FDI) related reforms that allowed easier access to foreign investors in the Indian market. These included permitting 100 per cent foreign investment in sectors such as horticulture, single-brand retail trading and food processing, among others. More recently in the Union Budget of 2016–17, the government proposed to allow 100 per cent FDI through Foreign Investment Promotion Board (FIPB) route in marketing of food products produced and manufactured in India.[5]

The Indian government has launched several national level schemes and initiatives to support the growth and development of food logistics business. One such initiative is the 'Make in India' campaign, encouraging foreign investors to invest in manufacturing facilities in sectors such as packaging. There are other initiatives such as 'Skill India' initiative that is dedicated to upgrading the existing skill levels in the country and 'Start-up India' initiative, which aim to support start-ups and commercialisation of R&D. All these measures and initiatives are likely to attract foreign companies, including companies from the United Kingdom (UK), to invest in India's food supply chain.

During his visit to the UK in November 2015, the Indian Prime Minister made a strong pitch to the UK companies to invest in India. Several memorandum of understanding (MoUs) were signed to facilitate collaborations, partnerships and knowledge sharing between India and the UK at different levels (for example, between two governments, between industry associations, business-to-business [B2B] etc.). While a number of UK companies have shown interest to invest in India, export to India and collaborate with Indian companies, they are aware that the Indian market is very different from the developed country markets, particularly the UK and other European country markets, where they have gained substantial experiences. Therefore, they need to know the market. The following sub-section discusses the dynamics of Indian market with a focus on food sector in comparison to the UK market.

5. The FIPB is under the Department of Economic Affairs, Ministry of Finance, Government of India. All non-residents making investments in the capital of resident entities in the sectors specified under 'Government Route' have to take a prior approval from the FIPB.

Market Dynamics: India and the UK

Market dynamics are factors that affect the demand and supply of a product. They broadly include indicators such as: economic growth, level of development, production and consumption patterns, external policies and the share of trade in the gross domestic product (GDP), among others. India and the UK have several differences with respect to these indicators.

India is a large developing country, which has been exhibiting a high GDP growth rate. According to the International Monetary Fund (IMF), the Indian economy grew at an average annual rate of 7.3 per cent in the year 2015. The country is expected to grow at 7.6 per cent in 2016 and 2017, and it is projected to be the fastest growing economy among emerging markets, leaving behind China, Brazil and Mexico. Compared to this, the UK is a large economy from the developed part of the world, which grew at 2.2 per cent in 2015 and is projected to grow at the same rate in 2016 and 2017. While India has been growing at a faster rate than the UK, the latter is more advanced in terms of its infrastructure and overall development.

While India is one of the largest producers of many agricultural products, the food processing sector in the country is still at a nascent stage. Only around 2 per cent of the agricultural produce is processed and bulk of the processing is in the non-corporate sector. Compared to this, while the UK is not a large agricultural producer, it has a large processed food industry. Majority of the UK companies are in the corporate sector. In the food supply chain, both India and the UK have a large number of small and medium enterprises (SMEs), but SMEs in the UK have their niche clientele and are more technology-oriented than Indian SMEs.

Food wastage in the UK is at the consumer-end while in India it is in the supply chain. The food supply chain in India is fragmented, and is characterised by the presence of a large number of unorganised operators in each segment. As a result, transportation costs in India are very high and so are the wastages involved in food transport due to mishandling, lack of storage facilities, etc. Compared to India, the UK has a well-established food supply chain and sophisticated logistics infrastructure. Most large multi-brand retailers and wholesale cash and carry operators in the UK have their own, well-established food supply chain. Logistics companies in the UK are now investing in infrastructure such as ports (for instance, the Uniserve Group, an international freight and logistics company, is investing in Felixstowe Port) and have the ability to provide end-to-end logistics solution for food supply chain.

While India continues to face a high level of food price inflation, the UK is facing a food price deflation. In January 2016, in India, the reported increase in food price was 6.85 per cent while in the UK, food prices fell by 2.6 per cent in the same period.[6] In India, the food inflation is the result of sporadic shortages and demand and supply gaps.

Focusing on consumption, both India and the UK have a high share of consumption expenditure in GDP. In 2014, India's household total consumption expenditure was 59.3 per cent of GDP, while it was 64.7 per cent for the UK in the same period.[7] The consumption patterns and shopping behaviour for food in India and the UK are different. Post global slowdown, the UK consumers have become price conscious and conservative with respect to their shopping habits. Instead of buying in bulk from the hypermarkets, the consumers in the UK are now buying as per their requirement and as a result low cost retailers are doing better than the large supermarkets.

In India, food and grocery retail is largely unorganised and the Indian consumers continue to shop from either small mom-and-pop stores or from the local markets and street vendors. These local mom-and-pop stores offer substantial competition to the organised retailers. Thus, large supermarket and hypermarkets are facing competition from smaller sized outlets in the two countries. In India, consumers are experimenting with brands, new products and new modes of retail and distribution (such as e-retail). This has led to double digit growth of the food supply chain sector and this is one of the fast growing sectors in India.

In India and the UK, majority of the consumers for organised retailers or imported products are located in the metro or large cities such as Delhi, Mumbai and London. However, the consumption pattern in the two economies is different. While in India, there is a demand for freshly cooked food, in the UK people largely consume convenience food. Thus, while in India most of the shopping is related to purchase of fresh fruits and vegetables, in the UK it is mostly processed or semi-processed produce. Moreover, in the UK consumers are now moving away from frozen

6. Extracted from *http://www.tradingeconomics.com/* (accessed on 8 March 2016).

7. See *http://data.worldbank.org/indicator/NE.CON.PETC.ZS* (accessed on 7 March 2016).

and towards chilled food. Chilled food has a shorter shelf life but it takes less energy to cook as it cooks faster. In India, processed food faces high taxes which increase the price and discourages its consumption. In both India and the UK, urban consumers are moving towards organic produce and produce with high nutrition content.

Objective of this Study

Given this background, the objective of this study is to examine the scope for improving the efficiency of the food supply chain in India through collaborations and investment inflows from the UK. The study focuses on five areas of the food supply chain logistics, namely storage and warehousing, cold-chains, packaging technology, skill development and R&D. It provides an overview of each of these segments in India and the UK, examines the regulations, identifies the areas of collaborations and suggests a go-to-market strategy for the UK companies. The study examines the barriers in the select segments of the food supply chain and makes policy recommendations to ease the barriers and facilitate more collaboration and investment from the UK.

Methodology

The study is based on secondary information analysis and a primary survey in India and the UK. A stakeholder's consultation was organised in Mumbai (India) on 28 October 2015 to get feedback from the industry. Interactions were held with the UK and Indian companies in a buyer-seller meet organised jointly by the UK Trade and Investment (UKTI) and the UK India Business Council (UKIBC) in London. In addition, a series of webinars were organised by the UKTI and UKIBC.

Structure of the Report

The layout of the report is as follows. Sections 1–5 provide an analysis of the status of the five segments of the food supply chain, namely storage and warehousing, cold-chains, packaging technology, skill development and R&D, in India highlighting the current and potential areas of collaborations and investments from the UK. Section 6 presents the general and sector specific barriers while Section 7 presents the policy recommendation and the way forward to enhance trade, investment and collaboration with the UK.

Section 1

Storage and Warehousing in India

The terms storage and warehousing are often used synonymously. They are key components of the food supply chain, which store both perishable (for example, fruits and vegetables) and non-perishable (for example, rice) produce in normal or temperature-controlled chambers from the time of production to the time of consumption to ensure a continuous flow of goods in the market. Storage or warehousing can be used at any stage in the food supply chain. On the basis of commodities stored, warehouses can be broadly classified into different categories such as retail warehouses, warehouses for storing agricultural goods, cold storages and container freight stations (CFSs) or inland container depots (ICDs), free trade warehousing zones (FTWZs), among others.

Storage and warehousing are a critical component of the food supply chain considering that: a) production of food crops is seasonal, b) most food products are grown in select states and c) consumption takes place year-around and all across the country. Traditionally, warehouses were manually operated and used for storing goods and inventories. Now warehouses and storages have become automated, which facilitates tracking and management of inventories. Importance of storage and warehousing has significantly increased in the last few years due to development of hub-and-spoke business models, globalisation, emergence of global production networks and supply chains. The growth of organised retail and global multinationals has also led to the establishment of global distribution centre. Today, warehouses provide a number of value-added services such as sorting, labelling and repackaging. A number of studies have shown that efficiency of the warehouses in terms of inventory management and short lead times, among others, affects the profitability of the users—manufacturers, retailers and distributors (for details see Christopher et al., 2006; Baker, 2007; Koskinen and Hilmola, 2008; Hilletofth, 2009).

Since companies are now establishing presence across the globe, warehousing cost is a key component of the logistics costs. As a result, companies are now looking to reduce warehousing costs by enhancing the efficiency through warehouse management systems and skilled labour. Developed countries are mature markets for warehousing and storages, where most of the warehouses are mechanised and automated. In the United States (US), for instance, the warehousing costs have reduced from 8.3 per cent in the early 1980s to 2.8 per cent, owing to a highly mechanised and automated warehousing industry (Knight Frank, 2014). Developing countries such as India and China are fast growing markets for storage and warehouses due to the development of global production networks, large population base, rise in consumer demand and establishment of organised retail, among others. However, the logistics cost in these markets remain high and the logistics infrastructure including storage and warehousing capacities are low. Therefore, the developing countries are seeking investments and technology from advanced economies in developing state-of-the-art warehousing and storage facilities which will help them to reduce the logistics cost.

Given this background, the focus of this section is on storage and warehousing facilities for agricultural commodities and processed food in India. For agricultural products, warehouses can help reduce the seasonality of supply and ensure price stability as well as preserve the quality of the product. With respect to processed food, modern warehouses help in inventory management, maintaining standards set out by the regulatory body and help create a more efficient distribution system for the manufacturing and retailing companies. This section has four sub-sections. Sub-sections 1.1 and 1.2 provide an overview of the storage and warehousing sector in the UK and India based on secondary literature. This is followed by (sub-section 1.3) a primary survey-based analysis on the warehouse and storage sector in India. The last section discusses the potential areas for collaboration and provides a 'go-to-market' strategy for foreign companies.

1.1 Brief Background of the Storage and Warehousing Sector in the UK

The global warehousing and storage industry has witnessed significant growth over the last few years and is expected to continue to grow to reach an estimated United States Dollar (USD)[1] 709.7 billion in 2017 with a compound annual growth rate (CAGR) of 5.8 per cent between 2012 and 2017 (Lucintel, 2012).While the share of warehousing in the logistics segment varies across countries, in the European Union (EU) it is around a quarter. Among the European countries, the UK is a key player in the warehousing and storage sector, holding almost 13 per cent of the total market in terms of distribution centres, sharing the second position alongside France [International Netherlands Group (ING) and Institute of Transport and Maritime Management Antwerp (ITMMA), 2012]. For food and beverages specifically, the main distribution centre in Europe are the Netherlands (36%), France (13%) and

1. All dollar values are in the United States (US) Dollar, unless specified otherwise.

Belgium (11%) while the UK is ranked fifth alongside Spain with 8 per cent share.

In the UK, the warehousing industry's revenue has grown at a steady pace of 2.1 per cent per annum from 2011 to 2015. Industry revenue is expected to grow at a compound annual rate of 2.1 per cent over the five years through 2015-16 to reach Great Britain Pound (GBP) 13.2 billion (USD 18.4 billion[2]).[3] In the recent past, most of the EU countries including the UK have seen a rise in the investment in warehouses, which has been fuelled primarily by the growth of online retail and e-commerce.

The storage and warehousing sector in the UK is governed by several statutory and non-statutory regulations. Any regulations related to food safety standards at the EU level or in the UK are applicable to agriculture warehousing sector in the UK. There are several other bodies and associations which also provide guidelines and standards for storage and warehousing. For example, the Agriculture and Horticulture Development Board, UK, has come up with a Grain Storage Manual in August 2011.[4]

The warehouse regulations are not just limited to construction and operations but they also cover health and safety of the workers in the warehouses. The UK government has provided companies with occupational health and safety[5] guidelines for the storage and warehousing industry. These guidelines are aimed at both employers and employees of those in the storage and warehousing industry, as well as those who work at or around warehouses in the course of their jobs, such as hauliers and couriers. The guidelines detail out the main causes of injury and ill health in storage and warehousing; how to manage risk of injuries and ill health in storage and warehousing especially for operating heavy machinery, working at heights, carriage of dangerous goods, among others.

At the international level, the International Organization for Standardization (ISO) have standards for warehousing, which are followed by a number of multinationals in the UK including Kraft Foods Group, Inc. and Mondelez International, Inc.

2. GBP 1 = USD 1.39 as per the currency conversion rate on 2 March 2016 accessed from *www.oanda.com* (accessed on 2 March 2016).
3. See *http://www.ibisworld.co.uk/market-research/warehousing-storage.html* (accessed on 7 October 2015).
4. Agriculture and Horticulture Development Board (2011).
5. See *http://www.hse.gov.uk/logistics/warehousing.htm* (accessed on 8 October 2015).

There are several active storage and warehousing associations in the UK. The International Federation of Warehousing & Logistics Associations,[6] located in London, promotes the logistics and warehousing industry. The association has members across the globe including India, China, Japan and Canada. From India, the National Association of Warehousing Corporations and the Central Warehousing Corporation (CWC) are members of the International Federation of Warehousing & Logistics Associations. The United Kingdom Warehousing Association (UKWA[7]) represents the third party logistics (3PL) sector. It acts as a mediator between various government departments and agencies, the European Commission and the logistics industry. The membership of this association is not restricted to just warehousing or logistics players; other stakeholders can also join. It also works on promoting the warehousing and logistics industry as well as setting and raising standards of the industry through international best practices. In order to become a member of UKWA, a company has to meet certain criteria including health and safety measures, fire protection measures and equipments, specialised storage amenities and handling and storage equipments, among others. A majority of the members are small and medium companies and many of these are exploring the Indian market.

1.2 Storage and Warehousing Sector in India

This sub-section discusses the key trends and developments in the Indian storage and warehousing sector, the types of storage and warehouses in India, prevalent regulations affecting the sector and the incentives offered by the government for the development of the sector.

1.2.1 Trends and Developments in the Sector

Traditionally, the storage and warehousing sector in India was characterised by a mere four-wall-and-shed establishment with sub-optimal size, inadequate ventilation and lighting, and poor hygienic conditions that lacked inventory management facilities. A majority of warehouses were used just as a stocking area for bulk distribution. At present, there is a shift towards modern warehouses and storage facilities, especially at the manufacturing and retail end, with automated warehouse management systems, where intermediate and manufactured goods are collected, assorted, stored

6. For details see their *website: http://www.ifwla.com/* (accessed on 12 October 2015).
7. For details see their website: *http://www.ukwa.org.uk/* (accessed on 18 October 2015).

and distributed to the point of consumption/sale. The non-perishable agricultural raw materials continue to be stored in traditional non-automated warehouses. Perishable products largely move through cold-chain which is discussed in Section 2.

A number of studies [see PricewaterhouseCoopers, (2011), Ernst & Young and Confederation of Indian Industry (CII), (2013), and Knight Frank (2014)] have projected a growth of 9-10 per cent for the industry. According to Ernst & Young and CII (2013), the size of the Indian warehousing industry (across commodities and modes) is pegged at around Indian National Rupee (INR) 560 billion (excluding inventory carrying cost, which amounts to another INR 4,340 billion) and is expected to grow 10 per cent annually over the next five years.[8] India's warehousing requirement is expected to grow at an annual average rate of 9 per cent from 919 million square feet (sq. ft.) in 2014 to 1,439 million sq. ft. in 2019. Among other segments, agricultural warehousing constitutes 15 per cent of the overall warehousing industry in India (see Figure 1.1), and is growing at a rate of 10-12 per cent since the financial year (FY)[9] 2010.[10]

Figure 1.1

Size of Different Sub-segments of the Indian Warehousing Industry in FY 2013 (in INR Million)

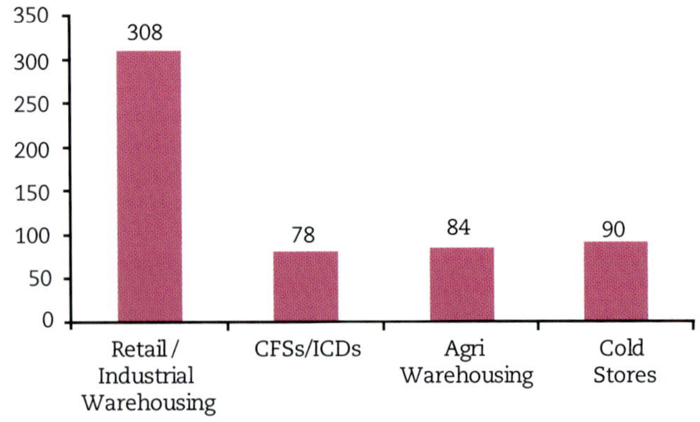

Source: Compiled from Ernst & Young and CII (2013).

Retail warehousing, which constitutes 55 per cent of the overall warehousing sector, has been growing at a CAGR of 10-12 per cent (Ernst & Young and CII, 2013). Entry of organised retailers (both domestic and foreign) and processed food manufacturers such as Reliance Retail, Future Group, Trent Limited, Aditya Birla Retail Limited, and PepsiCo India has led to a higher demand for high-end services and infrastructure as part of their overall supply chain requirements. Another form of storage and warehousing that is witnessing impressive growth is CFSs/ICDs. It constitutes about 14 per cent of the warehousing industry in India and is valued at INR 78 billion in FY 2013. CFSs and ICDs are the one of the rapidly growing segments of the logistics industry (Ernst & Young and CII, 2013), and have grown at a CAGR of around 15 per cent over the past 3 years and will continue to grow at a CAGR of 12-15 per cent over the next 4-5 years.

There are several drivers of this growth. As discussed earlier, Indian economy has been exhibiting a high growth rate and rise in consumer demand. This has also been reflected in the growth rate of allied sectors such as logistics. Along with strong macroeconomic parameters, there are several other drivers of growth of the storage and warehousing sector. Some of these are:

- *Growing agricultural production:* Foodgrains production in India has increased from 197 million tonnes in 2000-01 to 265 million tonnes (MT) in 2013-14.[11] With an increase in production of foodgrains, the year-on-year demand for storage has also increased. Consequently, the agri-warehousing sector has been growing at a CAGR of 8-10 per cent since FY 2010-11.[12] The total agri-warehousing capacity in India is about 109 MT as against the total demand of about 180 MT. To fill the gap, the Planning Commission has estimated creation of storage space of 35 million tonnes for foodgrains during 12th Five Year Plan (2012-2017).[13] The National Bank for Agriculture and Rural Development (NABARD) was allocated INR 50 billion in 2013-14 for supporting creation of infrastructure for storage of agricultural commodities.[14] In 2014, NABARD sanctioned INR 11.12 billion for creation of 1,336 warehouses under state governments and State Government Corporations in Haryana, Kerala, Punjab, Gujarat, Tamil Nadu, Tripura and West Bengal. The project

8. Ernst & Young and CII (2013). Available on *http://www.ey.com/Publication/vwLUAssets/The-Indian-Warehousing-Industry-An-Overview/USDFILE/EY-The-Indian-Warehousing-Industry-An-Overview.pdf* (accessed on 23 November 2015).
9. The Financial Year (FY) refers to the Indian financial year, which spans from 1st April to 31st March of every year.
10. *op. cit.* no. 8.
11. *http://eands.dacnet.nic.in/PDF/Agricultural-Statistics-At-Glance2014.pdf* (accessed on 19 November 2015).
12. *op. cit.* no. 8.
13. *https://www.nabard.org/pdf/PressRelease310114.doc* (accessed on 19 November 2015).
14. *https://www.nabard.org/english/NABARD_WAREHOUSING_SCHEME_NWS_2013_14.aspx* (accessed on 3 March 2016).

sanctioned under the NABARD Warehousing Scheme is expected to create an additional scientific storage space of 7.49 lakh MT for agricultural commodities.[15]

- *Changing consumption pattern and nature of food retail:* India has varied topography and different regions produce different products. However, consumption takes place throughout the country and in order to ensure availability, there is a need for storage and warehousing techniques that can hold the commodities longer and are located close to the consumption centres. This has motivated businesses to invest in the sector. Within retail, food retailing is the largest portion constituting 60 per cent of the total market. While the sector is largely non-corporate in nature, the share of organised retail is gradually rising. India's food retail sector is driven by changing consumption patterns along with fast changing demographics and habits, rising income and demand for quality products. Increased participation from foreign and private players will further boost the retail infrastructure in India and penetration of organised retail to tier-2 and tier-3 cities is likely to augment the demand for warehousing in India.

- *Growing international trade/containerised cargo:* Container traffic in the country has grown at a CAGR of 15 per cent as compared to 8 per cent globally, driving its share of global container traffic from 0.6 per cent in 1991 to 1.8 per cent in 2012.[16] Growth in containerised cargo traffic has facilitated the development of CFSs and ICDs, which have emerged as important components of the export-import value chain.

- *Increased investments in infrastructure:* There is an increased focus on completion of large-scale infrastructure projects like the Delhi Mumbai Industrial Corridor (DMIC) and the dedicated freight corridor (DFC). This is likely to generate huge demand for warehouses, thereby giving a significant boost to warehousing and logistics-related real estate demand. The railways also have opened up for private investments in the form of public private partnerships (PPPs) with respect to private container train operators. Other than these, new ports, inland container terminals, CFSs, and FTWZs have come up/are coming up, which is likely to give a boost to storage and warehousing sector in India.

- *Easing of foreign investment regulations:* The Indian government has initiated several FDI-related reforms. For instance, the government has allowed 100 per cent FDI in a large number of sectors including storage and warehousing, manufacturing, retailing, etc. In addition, several FDI-related rules have been eased. This gives a fresh impetus to foreign businesses to invest in the sector, thereby driving the growth.

Although, in the past, government (at both the centre and state) and government agencies played a key role in the development of warehouses and storage facilities, primarily for storages of foodgrains, in the recent years there has been an increase in private participation and PPP models due to several government incentives. With the entry of private players, the composition of the storage and warehousing sector is changing and the warehouses are becoming more automated and sophisticated. The next sub-section highlights the type and nature of storage and warehouses in India.

1.2.2 Type of Warehouses in India

Warehouses in India are classified based on their ownership and the type of commodity they hold. By ownership they can be: a) owned by the central or state governments, b) developed or managed under a PPP model and c) privately owned. By commodities, they can store perishable and non-perishable agricultural produce. Warehouses can be single-product or multi-product. They can be temperature controlled with options of multi-chamber temperature control. Temperature-controlled warehouses are referred to as cold storages and are discussed in Section 2. Warehouses are also classified based on whom they cater to. For example, FTWZs mostly cater to trade—exports and imports.

As mentioned earlier, in India, a majority of the storage and warehousing sector is owned and controlled by the government or is under the public sector. The total warehousing capacity available in India in public sector, cooperative and private sector is about 117.82 million tonnes, the details of which are given in Table

15. *http://www.business-standard.com/article/economy-policy/nabard-sanctions-rs-1-112-cr-for-creation-of-1-336-warehouses-in-7-states-114020401256_1.html* (accessed on 3 March 2016).
16. *https://www.kpmg.com/IN/en/IssuesAndInsights/ArticlesPublications/Documents/KPMG_All_Aboard_Insights_into_India_maritime_community.pdf* (accessed on 4 November 2015).

1.1. Government agencies such as Food Corporation of India (FCI) are key users of the warehouses. Warehouses in India are largely utilised for the storage of foodgrains procured for the central pool. Some of the private storage capacity is also hired by the government agencies for storage of stocks of foodgrains. Other agricultural commodities like pulses, oil seeds, spices, condiments, dry fruits, sugar, etc. are stored by CWC, State Warehousing Corporations (SWCs) and private warehouses. Foodgrain storage is also demanded by commodity exchanges such as Multi Commodity Exchange Limited and National Commodity and Derivative Exchange, which use private godowns and warehouses for storage of commodities that are listed on the exchange.

Table 1.1

Storage Capacity of Warehouses by Ownership

Organisation/Sector	*Storage Capacity (in million metric tonnes)*
Food Corporation of India (FCI)	38.34
State Warehousing Corporations (SWC) and State Agencies	34.84
Private Sector	18.97
Cooperative Sector	15.37
Central Warehousing Corporation (CWC)	10.30
Total	117.82

Source: Extracted from Section 2.2 of the Warehousing Development & Regulatory Authority (2014). Available at *http://wdra.nic.in/Annual%20Report%20(english)%202013-2014.pdf* (accessed on 28 March 2016).

As mentioned earlier, traditionally the warehouses in India were non-corporate and small in size. This is due to a number of factors. First, a number of incentives are given by the government to SMEs to build warehouses. This has resulted in a number of players having 1-2 warehouses. Second, to avoid paying central sales tax and due to the differences in state sales taxes, companies prefer to use separate warehouses in every state and they hardly operate on a hub-and-spoke model. Third, the government warehouses as per the guidelines designed by the Warehousing Development and Regulatory Authority (WDRA) require minimal automation and are dependent on manual labour for loading, unloading and commodity handling.[17] Therefore, the warehouse developers tend to meet the basic requirements and do not spend on automation to keep the cost low. Manpower cost is much lower in India compared to countries such as the UK. Fourth, most of the users of warehouses such as retailers, farmers are small and non-corporate companies. Globally, organised retailers and manufacturers are the drivers of modern warehouses as they need fast and efficient inventory management. In India, the presence of organised retailers and manufacturers in food products is low. Overall, the sporadic development of warehouses with minimalistic infrastructural facilities has resulted in not only lack of economies of scale but also wastage and pilferages.

Overtime, private participation in warehousing has increased with the entry of domestic corporate and multinational corporations. The government has initiated schemes such as the Mega Food Park Scheme under which private sectors are given grant for making food parks, which include storage and warehouses. Some other schemes of the government are discussed in the later sub-sections. The development of FTWZs and agro-logistics parks has also supported the growth of this sector. Even in the case of foodgrains, the entry of corporates and retailers who brought in premium brands such as India Gate basmati rice (by Khushi Ram Behari Lal Limited) and Pillsbury Atta (by General Mills India), has created a demand for modern warehousing facilities.

A number of warehousing service providers have emerged who are now providing integrated services such as warehousing and trucking, or warehousing and cold-chains, or warehousing and storage, with value-added services such as break bulk handling, inventory management and custom clearances. For instance, Adani Agri Logistics, Star Agri Warehousing & Collateral Management Limited and Shree Shubham Logistics Limited have pan-India operations. While some companies operate their own warehouses, there are others that provide warehouse management services. A number of start-ups have also been launched in the sector, which are discussed later. In order to make their warehouses more competitive, these companies are focussing on incorporating better technology and allied services like testing and transportation, moving towards integrating the various parts of the supply chain.

1.2.3 Regulations Affecting the Indian Storage and Warehousing Sector

As mentioned earlier, the government has played a significant role in fostering the growth of the storage

17. The various guidelines imposed by WDRA can be found in the following links: *http://wdra.nic.in/Notifications/gz2.pdf* (accessed on 31 March 2016); *http://wdra.nic.in/Notifications/gz4.pdf* (accessed on 31 March 2016); *http://wdra.nic.in/Notifications/Regulations%202015%20English.pdf* (accessed on 31 March 2016); *http://wdra.nic.in/Notifications/gz6.pdf* (accessed on 31 March 2016); *http://wdra.nic.in/Notifications/gz8.pdf* (accessed on 31 March 2016).

and warehousing market in India. The government regulations, schemes and taxes are at two separate levels—the centre and the state. At the centre, 100 per cent FDI is allowed under automatic route in storage and warehousing including warehousing of agricultural products with refrigeration (cold storage) and the tax structure has also been reframed to make the sector more lucrative for investments. There have been several initiatives to promote investments by the private sector in Special Economic Zones (SEZs), logistics parks and mega food parks (MFPs). Support infrastructures such as the DFCs, industrial corridors and port facilities have been developed or are currently under the process of development in order to integrate the overall supply chain.

One of the most significant policy milestones in the warehousing and storage sector was the establishment of WDRA through the Warehousing (Development and Regulation) Act, in September 2007. The role of WDRA is to regulate and ensure implementation of the provisions of the Warehousing (Development and Regulation) Act, 2007, regulate negotiability of warehouse receipts and promote orderly growth of the warehousing business.

As of July 2015, 949 warehouses were registered with WDRA including warehouses of CWC, SWCs, private warehouses and cooperative societies.[18] Since the warehouses need to be registered and accredited by WDRA, the companies or individuals have to follow certain specifications for building and operating the warehouses. The Warehouse Manual for Operationalizing of Warehousing (Development & Regulation) Act, 2007, states that the warehouse must be constructed as per Bureau of Indian Standards (BIS)/CWC/FCI standards/specification.[19]

The main objectives of the Warehousing (Development and Regulation) Act, 2007 are to make provisions for the development and regulation of warehouses, negotiability of warehouse receipts, and the establishment of WDRA and related matters. It was expected that the negotiable warehouse receipts issued by the warehouses registered under this Act would help the farmers to seek loans from banks against the negotiable warehouse receipts and this would in turn help avoid the distress sale of agricultural produce. It was also expected to be beneficial to a number of other stakeholders such as banks, financial institutions, insurance companies, trade, commodities exchanges as well as consumers.

It is worth mentioning that unlike the case of India, the UK does not have a specific regulation for warehouses. In the UK, the government does not own or control the warehouses as it is done in India. In the UK, warehouses are privately owned and managed. Moreover, in the UK, many warehouses take the ISO certificate or the British Retail Consortium (BRC) Global Standard certificate. These certificates are recognised by global multinational manufactures and retailers and are taken as a benchmark for quality standards. Only a few storages and warehouses in India have globally recognised certificates. These certificates are important especially for companies engaged in trade and establishment of global production networks.

1.2.4 Schemes and Incentives in India

Agriculture is a priority sector for the Indian government. Agri-warehousing, being a part of the agricultural supply chain, also comes under the priority sector for the government. From time to time, the government has come up with different schemes to support the development of warehouses (see Table 1.2). In 2014-15, the government allocated INR 50 billion to NABARD to develop agri-storage infrastructure across the country.[20] Agri-warehousing activity is covered under 'Priority Sector Lending' by the central bank, Reserve Bank of India (RBI).[21]

Table 1.2 provides an overview of the storage and warehousing sector in India. It highlights the scope for private investments in the sector. To understand the present operating environment and the scope for future investments and foreign collaborations in the storage and warehousing sector, a primary survey has been conducted. The survey findings are presented in the next section.

18. *http://wdra.nic.in/State-wise%20List%20of%20the%20Warehouses%20Registered%20with%20WDRA.pdf* (accessed on 18 November 2015).

19. *http://wdra.nic.in/WAREHOUSEMANUAL30012013.pdf* (accessed on 18 November 2015).

20. *https://www.nabard.org/english/NABARD_WAREHOUSING_SCHEME_NWS_2013_14.aspx* (accessed on 19 November 2015).

21. Priority sector refers to those sectors of the economy, which may not get timely and adequate credit in the absence of this special dispensation. Priority Sector Lending is an important role given by the Reserve Bank of India (RBI) to the banks for providing a specified portion of the bank lending to few specific sectors like agriculture and allied activities, micro and small enterprises, poor people for housing, students for education and other low income groups and weaker sections. The rate of interest on various priority sector loans will be as per RBI's directives issued from time to time, which is linked to base rate of banks at present. Priority sector guidelines do not lay down any preferential rate of interest for priority sector loans.

Table 1.2

Select Central Government Schemes for Warehouses and Storages

Scheme Name	*Inception*	*Nodal Ministry*	*Purpose*
Private Entrepreneurs Guarantee Scheme	2008	Ministry of Consumers Affairs, Food & Public Distribution	To take care of increasing levels of production/procurement of foodgrains and to reduce the dependence on Cover and Plinth (CAP) type of open storage for foodgrains. The Department of Food & Public Distribution is implementing the scheme for augmenting the storage capacity of FCI through PPP mode. The Department would implement creation of additional storage capacity for foodgrains through private sector, CWC and SWCs. Till October 2015, 130 lakh MT capacity has been completed and 152 lakh MT has been sanctioned.[b]
Construction of modern warehousing (silos) facilities through PPP	As of November 2015, tenders were floated and bids would soon be finalised[a]	Ministry of Consumers Affairs, Food & Public Distribution	As part of the Private Entrepreneurs Guarantee Scheme, the PPP model has been proposed to be used for creating integrated modern storage facilities for wheat in the form of silos. A few silos will also be constructed for storage of rice on experimental basis. FCI prepared an Action Plan for constructing total 100 Lakh MT silos in a phased manner, including some silos through state governments and other agencies. FCI has identified 6 locations *viz.*, Changsari (Assam), Narela (Delhi), Sahnewal (Punjab), Kotkapura (Punjab), Katihar (Bihar) and Whitefield (Karnataka) where land is available with rail siding in existing premises.[c] The private entrepreneurs would be eligible for Viability Gap Funding (VGF), where land would be provided by FCI/state governments. For storage of wheat in these silos, the developer will be entitled to receive a recurring service charge, provided he meets the required performance and maintenance standards. Where land is not available with FCI/government, silos would be constructed in non-VGF mode.
Agricultural Marketing Infrastructure (AMI)	2014 (Grameen Bhandharan Yojana (implemented in 2001) and Scheme for Development / Strengthening of Agricultural Marketing Infrastructure, Grading & Standardisation (implemented in 2004) merged to form AMI)	NABARD - Department of Refinance (Ministry of Finance)	To provide infrastructural facilities for grading, standardising, and quality certification for agricultural produce, to develop agricultural marketing infrastructure for effectively managing marketable surplus of agriculture and allied sectors including dairy, poultry, fishery, etc., to promote innovative and latest technologies in agricultural marketing infrastructure, to promote direct marketing so as to increase market efficiency through reduction in intermediaries and hand ling channels so as to increase farmers' incomes, to promote integrated value chains, etc.[d] The scheme provides for subsidy of 25 per cent, but for North East States & Farmers Producers Organisations, *panchayats*, women scheduled cast and scheduled tribes , Self Help Group, the subsidy is 33.33 per cent. Since its inception, storage capacity of around 51 million MT has been sanctioned and 37.05 million MT storage capacity has already been created under this scheme.
Scheme for Financing Warehousing Infrastructure under Rural Infrastructure Development Fund/ Warehousing Infrastructure Fund (RIDF/ WIF)	WIF in 2014-2015 RIDF in the 1995-1996 Union Budget	NABARD - Department of Refinance (Ministry of Finance)	The WIF envisages extension of loans to public and private sectors for construction of warehouses, silos, cold storages and other cold-chain infrastructure. It would be utilised for meeting the growing demand for scientific storage capacity for agricultural commodities in the entire country. Priority will be given to the projects proposed in Eastern and North Eastern states and foodgrain deficit states. Loans will be provided for proposals of projects involving creation of storage infrastructure, with a minimum aggregate capacity of 5000 MT, for agricultural and allied produce.[e] RIDF was instituted in NABARD with an announcement in the Union Budget 1995-1996 with the sole objective of giving low cost fund support to State Governments and State Owned Corporations for quick completion of ongoing projects relating to medium and minor irrigation, soil conservation, watershed management and other forms of rural infrastructure.[f]

Note: a: *http://dfpd.nic.in/peg.htm* (accessed on 22 March 2016); b. *http://dfpd.nic.in/peg-storage-scheme.htm* (accessed on 22 March 2016); c. *http://dfpd.nic.in/peg.htm* (accessed on 22 March 2016); d. *https://www.nabard.org/pdf/AMI_Website.pdf* (accessed on 22 March 2016); e. *https://www.nabard.org/pdf/Website_Warehouse_Infrastructure_Fund_WIF_2014_15.pdf* (accessed on 22 March 2016); f. *https://www.nabard.org/english/GenesisRIDF.aspx* (accessed on 22 March 2016).

Source: Compiled from the websites of NABARD and the Department of Food & Public Distribution (Ministry of Consumer Affairs, Food & Public Distribution).

1.3 Findings of the Primary Survey

The Dun & Bradstreet Tangram Advisory Services Private Limited has conducted 27 in-depth interviews with the Indian and UK companies engaged in the storage and warehousing sector, warehouse specific industry associations, FCI, CWC, and policymakers in India and the UK. The survey also includes three MFPs to understand the role and scope of storage and warehousing in integrated food parks. The questions are focused on the business model of the companies, their perception about the current growth and future potential of the sector in India, technology gap and areas for collaboration with the UK, barriers that they are facing or are likely to face, their expectation from the government, among others.

The survey findings are compiled under four sub-sections below: the business model or the operating structure of the existing players, technology usage at present facilities and the gap, the scope for training and the future growth potential. The responses on barriers and reforms requirements are summarised in Sections 6 and 7, respectively.

1.3.1 The Business Model

The survey shows that the agri-warehouse requirements are primarily from two categories of users/customers—the government and the private companies (who comprise mainly food processors and retailers). There is a third category of warehouse users who store agriculture produce for commodity trading.

The warehouses that serve the government are mostly leased out to FCI for foodgrain storage. FCI procures foodgrains on behalf of the government with the primary aim of food security. Currently, FCI has three types of warehouses—covered godowns, silos and CAP.[22] All the warehouses of FCI are used for foodgrain storage and majority of the warehouses are not automated.

Another public sector entity, CWC, is one of the biggest warehousing providers to FCI. During the survey it is pointed out that CWC has around 470 warehouses across the country with a total capacity of more than 10 million MT. CWC also leases out its warehousing space to private players at differential pricing. Specifically, CWC charges from FCI on per quintal/month basis while it charges on square meter basis from the private clients. FCI gives INR 3.38 per quintal/month as rental of godowns/warehouses to CWC. This rent remains same irrespective of the location being used by FCI. Compared to this, the rental charged by CWC from private clients is about four to five times higher than what is charged from FCI.

As in the case of FCI warehouses, majority of the CWC warehouses lack automation. When enquired, both FCI and CWC pointed out that there is no need for automation in the warehouses since they are only used to store the foodgrains and the bags of grains can be manually stacked one above the other. Moreover, with automation, there is lesser space available for storing the grain bags as space has to be created for movement of cranes. Further, the survey confirms that labour costs are low and therefore, the cost of non-automated warehouses are low. The warehouses of CWC that are used for storing industrial goods by the private customers are automated. The survey also confirms that the demand from the users will drive the process of automation and technological upgradation in warehouses in India.

The private players in warehouses offer different kinds of services. While some offer warehousing facilities to FCI and SWC for storage of foodgrains, there are others who cater to commodity trading and a third group caters to processed food items and retail clients.

The private warehouses catering to FCI, CWC and state government or commodity exchanges are most likely to be manual with basic infrastructure. However, they all adhere to the specifications laid down by FCI/CWC/BIS. The monthly rentals of the warehouses catering to FCI are fixed by FCI and are based on per quintal of the quantity stored.

There are warehousing service providers for multiple agricultural commodities including special commodity warehouses for storing cotton, pulses, maize, spices, foodgrains, and castor seeds, etc. While some of these players invest in creating their own infrastructure, others take the space on long-term lease/hire basis. They offer various kinds of services to their clients. For example, with a pan-India network of over 800 warehouses across 16 states and over 1.5 million tonnes of warehousing capacity, Star Agri-Warehousing offers integrated post-harvest solution to both buyers and producers/farmers. Apart from warehousing, it offers collateral financing, procurement and value-added services to enhance efficiency across the entire food supply chain. Sohal Lal Commodities Management Private Limited is an ISO certified agri-logistics company which offers comprehensive warehousing services (including warehouse management services, agri-financing, collateral management and post harvest procurement services) for over 366 agricultural commodities.

Additionally, there are the state-of-the-art warehouse service providers catering to the needs of food retailers and processed food manufacturers. The organised food retail industry in India is growing at a faster pace and so is the need for a warehousing management system. The warehouses catering to the retailers, exporters and manufacturers have modern technology and they offer various value-added services including sorting, grading, packaging, weighing, testing and inspection, among others.

The survey confirms that storage and warehousing sector in India is marked by the presence of small and mid-sized fragmented operators, who compete on lower costs. While most of the players meet the standards/specifications as set by FCI/CWC/BIS for building and construction of a warehouse, very few invest in automation or mechanisation of the storage spaces. Considering that the share of organised retail is growing in India, there is likely to be a greater need for automated warehouses in the future. The large

22. A CAP is one where stock is kept on the plinth and covered with polythene covers.

private companies in this sector are keen on foreign collaborations which will enable them to not only expand but have access to global best practices.

1.3.2 Technology Usage

Most of the agri-warehouses in India are not automated and they only meet the basic standards set by the regulator. The design of the warehouse largely depends on the end-user requirements. Majority of them use brick, mortar and pre-fabricated panels. For these, the buildings can primarily be of two kinds, pre-engineered buildings or reinforced concrete cement buildings. These warehouses are used to store foodgrains. They are designed so that it is easy to stack gunny bags that store the foodgrain manually. To maximise the storage space, there are no racks or compartments and the bags are stored on top of each other.

Storage in such warehouses can lead to wastage and pilferage. For example, the survey has found that if there is a lot of pressure from the top or if the bags soak moisture it can tear the bag. Fumigation, which forms an important process for keeping the produce pest free, is also ignored in many warehouses. To counter problems of moisture generation in the warehouses, some warehouses have ventilation facilities. However, this can lead to entry of pests and insects into the warehouses.

In recent years, the government has focused on use of silos for storage of rice and wheat. Attempts are being made by FCI to create state-of-the-art foodgrains storage facilities and silos through private sector participation.[23] Silos have several benefits. They require lesser space/land (around one-third of land is required as compared to the traditional structures) and offer better safety and lock the quality of the stored items. They also enable better monitoring and overall reduce grain wastages.[24] They have greater storage capacity that results in efficiency in production and distribution of grains. However, silos require uniform grain quality and are suitable for large agricultural produce of homogenous variety.

Compared to this, retail, multi-commodity warehouses, CFSs and ICDs are automated. The clients of such warehouses require equipment such as cranes and technology such as radio frequency identification (RFID) trackers. Processed food needs to be stored in racks. The clients/users need technology and efficient warehouse designs for inventory management and tracking and reduction in wastages and pilferages. With the introduction of quick service restaurants (QSRs) and fast moving consumer goods (FMCG), warehouses now need to act as high response centres. These warehouses also require technology and skilled workforce for operating machinery or for inventory management.

Almost all respondents have pointed out that there is sufficient storage capacity in India; however, the issue lies in the poor quality and lack of management of the warehouses and the non-uniform spread of warehouses across different states. As the demand for warehouses is rising, there is a growing realisation for improving the warehouse management system. As pointed earlier, many of the private players interviewed work on a lease model rather than owning the facility. Hence, the warehouses are hired or leased closer to the client site or requirement. Their business model is asset light but uses technology for better and efficient management of warehouses.

Technology can be a powerful tool for gaining competitive advantage and many companies are designing programmes which can help in warehouse management. As a result, there is an increase in the productivity and the efficiency of the warehouse. A complete warehouse management system incorporates picking, inventory control, label printing, return material authorisation, receiving and automatic data collection and much more. Box 1.1 shows an example of technology and programmes by an Indian company. In order to increase efficiency, the organised players have realised that structure, location, support infrastructure, technology and connectivity are key to the success of the warehouse business. A number of start-up companies have entered this segment bringing in new technologies to improve connectivity in the supply chain and reduce wastages. Among them, Star Agri, Shree Shubham Logistics, Sohan Lal Commodity Management, Siddhivinayak Agri Processing, INI Farms, and Allfresh deserve a special mention. While some of these cater to specific product categories, others operate across a wide range of produce. A number of these start-ups operate at the grass-root level directly with the farmers. For example, EM3 Agri Services helps in land preparation and crop harvesting on a 'pay-per-acre' basis to small land holdings at economical rates, while eFarm enables its clients to escape the chains of intermediaries by directly linking buyers with the sellers of agricultural

23. See also *http://fci.gov.in/app/webroot/upload/News/Report%20of%20the%20High%20Level%20Committee%20on%20Reorienting%20the%20Role%20and%20Restructuring%20of%20FCI_English.pdf* (accessed on 7 December 2015).

24. *http://www.fci.gov.in/app/webroot/upload/Storage/Silo%20Conference%20PPT.pdf* (accessed on 23 November 2015).

produce and allied services via a web and mobile-based portal. Reuters Market Light, Fasal Intuit and mKrish provide personalised agricultural market information (such as quality inputs, weather patterns, best prices, market access, etc.) to farmers through a mobile-based service (SMS or voice messages). Utilising information and communication technology (ICT) to provide logistics solutions is how Logistimo enables its clients to manage their inventory, credit, track truck deliveries and routing, monitor workforce behaviour and forecast demand through a mobile app.

There is also growing investment by private companies in logistics parks and multi-modal logistics hubs across India, which shows that companies are now trying to integrate the various segments of the supply chain. Also, there is an effort to consolidate the large number of fragmented and small warehouses into a few large integrated models, using information technology. Through these initiatives, the private players are moving towards a hub-and-spoke model.

The survey respondents have pointed out that efficiency will increase with economies of scale and government policies such as the single goods and services tax (GST), which will lead to scale expansion.

GST is expected to accelerate the growth of the storage and warehousing industry and creation of true hub-and-spoke model, which India currently lacks. Rolling out of GST is further expected to drive the technology adoption since under hub-and-spoke model technology will be of paramount importance.

Foodgrain Stack in FCI Godown.

Source: Taken from the web: *http://www.fci.gov.in/fci/img/uploads/Foodgrain%20stack%20in%20FCI%20Godown.JPG*

Sohan Lal Commodities Management Private Limited (SLCMs) warehouse for Agri Commodities.

Courtesy: SLCM Group.

Silos at Integrated Food Park Private Limited in Tumkur, Karnataka.

Source: Picture taken in 2014 during the Evaluation of the Impact of the Scheme for Mega Food Park of Ministry of Food Processing Industries.

1.3.3 Training

The survey has found that the training requirements vary with different types of storage and warehousing facilities. For the public sector warehouses, there is no specific training provided to the labour. For instance, one of the leading public sector warehousing players mentioned that the labour only learns on the job and there is no specific training provided to them. However, CWC and others provide training to the technical staff related to areas such as food safety standards, carrying out inspection of foodgrains, instructions for pest control and on how the bags are to be stacked. The overall training duration is for one year, which comprises three month classroom training and the remaining nine months on-the-job training. Curriculum of the training is designed based on the requirement.

Compared to this, the nature of training provided by the private warehouses differs to a large extent. While the curriculum consists of classroom training as well as on-the-job training, the employees are trained on the use of sophisticated warehousing management system and equipment like forklifts, etc. The level of training provided by them to their employees is entirely different. All of the private storage and

Box 1.1

Sohan Lal Commodities Management (SLCM) Private Limited

SLCM is a commodities management company that provides a range of services to its customers such as management of commodity warehouses, agri-financing, collateral management and procurement.

The company uses innovative techniques and modern technology for warehouse management and also provides other services such as financing. SLCM focuses on scientific warehousing processes rather than infrastructure creation and it manages a network of 780 warehouses across India. The uniqueness of the company is that it has systems to monitor warehouses located anywhere in the country through their technology enabled network. It does not require the personnel to be at the client site for monitoring the products. It was pointed out during the survey that they can even report the moisture levels in the grain without physically inspecting the products. They have a programme called 'Agri Reach', which is a proprietary technology developed by the group that enables the tracking of Real Time Data about Quality & Quantity of the commodities at the warehouses across India. It primarily uses android tablets for entering the data at warehouse locations. While the warehouse manager captures the data pertaining to inward/outward taking place at the warehouse, it simultaneously updates the data on the Systems, Applications and Products (SAP) Application server on Real Time Basis. This helps in effective monitoring of crop to take preventive and curative measures at the right time. The company claims that Agri Reach helps in reducing the wastages from 10 per cent to a mere 0.5 per cent. Moreover, all the warehouses under SLCM are geo-fenced which is a tool to track the on-field officers on a real-time basis. The company has been successful in raising four rounds of FDI. Apart from this, the company has a programme called 'Kassandhan' that offers financing solutions on agriculture collateral. Over a short span of time, the Kissandhan project disbursed INR 2.5 billion of loans, serviced over 9,770 storage receipts at 47 locations. This kind of initiative helps farmers avoid distress sales. SLCM has managed to affect about 30,000 farmers until March 2015.

Source: Findings during the survey and information collected from the website: *http://sohanlal.in/index.html* (accessed on 28 March 2016).

warehousing players contacted mention that they provide customised training to their employees based on the job requirement. For example, a forklift operator will be given classroom training as well as on-the-job training on how to move forklifts in a warehouse, how to use a forklift for loading/unloading, etc.

1.3.4 Future Growth Potential

Most of the survey respondents have highlighted that the storage capacity in India has reached near saturation in most states. There may be some requirement for storages and warehouses in hilly regions such as Jammu and Kashmir and in the North-East states of India. Therefore, the focus of the government has to move away from construction to automation and better management of warehouses and storages.

It is pointed out during the survey that the storage and warehousing players are expecting a growth of over 10 per cent over the next 3-4 years owing to multiple reasons including rolling out of GST, creation of hub-and-spoke structure, modernisation of existing facilities, etc. They also mentioned that the major scope for development lies in better technology through automations and warehouse management systems. Hence,there is a need for scientific warehouse management. This is a huge area for private investment and technology collaboration. The future growth of this sector will depend on the entry of domestic and foreign players in food manufacturing and retailing. While the government is encouraging manufacturers to invest in India, there are FDI restrictions in multi-brand retail. Removal of FDI restrictions in retail will be a key growth driver for this sector.

The next section discusses some of the other areas of collaboration and the market entry strategy for the UK businesses.

1.4 Existing and Potential Areas of Cooperation and Go-to-Market Strategy for the UK Companies

One of the key drivers of the warehousing sector in India will be high economic growth and increase in investment in infrastructure projects such as roads, railways, highways and expressways, and economic and industrial corridors. Several infrastructure projects are already underway such as DMIC and the other DFCs and there is a great scope of integrating the supply chain through these economic and industrial corridors. The UK companies can focus on development of warehouses along DFCs and economic corridors. It is important for the companies to identify the right state, the right location within the state and the right business partner.

The above analysis highlights that while there are sufficient number of warehouses in India, they lack sophisticated technology and management system. As a result, there is inefficiency in system and wastages. With the growth of organised retail sector, retail warehouses with technology and other automations are required. Information Technology (IT) plays a key role in supporting the storage and warehousing sector. According to NSDC,[25] there is a need for investment in infrastructure and mechatronic warehouses with sophisticated material handling equipment, racking and security systems to remain competitive. Investments in technology to provide real time, online connectivity by offering intelligent tracking of packages, pallets and vehicles are also required to achieve competitiveness.[26] Some of the areas where IT plays an important role include warehouse management systems, track and trace, enterprise resource planning, etc. Specifically, the survey has found that there is scope for investment by the UK companies in three key areas, namely warehouse management systems, RFID technology, and warehouse design and operating process design. There is scope for investment by the UK companies in reduction of wastages, better stacking and product handing systems, and in integrated logistics parks providing certain value-added services, FTWZs and agri-warehousing zones. The UK companies can explore the possibilities of setting up storages and warehousing facilities in food parks, including MFPs.

The changing trend of the Indian warehousing sector needs considerable amount of skilled and trained personnel. According to NSDC,[27] there is shortage of expertise in warehousing sector due to the lack of institutions providing training in logistics.[28] The report further states that the demand for human resource in the transportation, logistics, and warehousing sector is expected to increase from about 7.3 million in 2008-09 to about 25 million by 2022, leading to an incremental human resource requirement for about 17.7 million persons. There is scope for the UK companies to participate in skill development which is discussed in detail in Section 4.

There are several ways in which a foreign company can establish its presence in India. One of the most preferred routes for international businesses is through joint venture (JV). This is considered better than establishing a wholly owned subsidiary (WOS) as it helps the foreign company to gain the local market knowledge through local partnership. It can also enable them to use the existing network of the local partner. Another mode of entry is through mergers or acquisitions. In the case of India, a number of companies have grown through mergers and acquisitions.

The UK companies should be aware that India has a quasi-federal governance structure and the regulations related to logistics and distribution vary across states. Each state has different regulatory requirements—some easier than the others. Further, some states are large production centres for agricultural products while others are large consumption centres. Companies have to undertake proper feasibility study/market research before establishing presence, based on their requirements. Ideally, they should select a state, which is open to investors, willing to provide an atmosphere conducive to business development, a healthy production of crops and food processing sector.

It is found during the survey that knowledge and information about the Indian market is limited. Therefore, there is need for collaboration and knowledge sharing at the level of the industry associations in order to disseminate information about each other's market. While the UKIBC can handhold the companies at the stage of entry to the Indian market, the UK companies have pointed out that neither UKIBC nor UKWA has a detailed knowledge about the processes of entering into the Indian market, type of clearances that are required, etc. There is a need to understand the processes and difference in the processes across states. The companies are also keen to know how they can dovetail the benefits offered by the central and state governments.

The survey participants in the UK have pointed out that the present technology in India was prevalent in the UK almost 20 years back. Although there is a huge opportunity for the UK companies to invest in the sector and enable technology transfer, they may need to customise their technology to India's local market requirements. To begin with, the UK warehousing companies are more suited to cater to large Indian manufacturers, retailers and exporters. They have to identify some niche clientele.

India is a price sensitive market and there is stiff competition from the SMEs and the unorganised sector

25. *http://www.nsdcindia.org/sites/default/files/files/transportation-logistics-2009.pdf* (accessed on 23 November 2015).
26 Ibid. (assessed from page 23).
27 Ibid.
28 Ibid.

in the storage and warehousing segment. Therefore, the UK companies should have the right pricing model.

In conclusion, there is scope for investment and collaboration with the UK companies and industry associations in storage and warehousing sector. There is also scope for the Indian and UK companies to collaborate and leverage on their mutual strength to enter third country markets in the South Asian Association for Regional Cooperation (SAARC) region. However, the survey has found that there are several barriers to investment in the warehousing and storage sector which are discussed in Section 6. These need to be addressed to get the investments.

Section

2

Cold-chain Sector in India

> Cold-chain is a logistics system that provides a series of facilities to maintain ideal storage conditions for perishables from the point of origin to the point of consumption in the food supply chain (Planning Commission, 2012: 24, Section 1.9.13).

Cold-chain helps to increase the shelf life or holding life of the perishables. The cold-chain infrastructure is quite similar to a regular supply chain but additionally needs pack-houses with proper pre-cooling and packaging systems, refrigerated vehicles for primary and secondary transportation and cold storages. The refrigerated vehicles and cold storages are generally multi-chamber with multi-temperature controls to support the movement of perishables under ambient, produce, chill and frozen categories.

Cold-chains broadly cater to industries related to food and agriculture, chemical and pharmaceutical. Within food, the cold-chain caters to perishable produce. The primary segments of an integrated cold-chain include:

- Packing and cooling fresh food products;
- Cold storage (short or long term warehousing of chilled or frozen foods);
- Distribution (cold transport and temporary warehousing under temperature-controlled conditions), and
- Marketing (refrigerated or freezer storage and displays at wholesale markets, retail markets and food service operations).

In terms of market size, globally, the meat and seafood markets account for the largest share of products being supported by cold-chain infrastructure, followed by dairy and frozen desserts, and fruits and vegetables. With liberalisation of agriculture trade and development of processed food industry, cross-country movement of fresh and processed products has increased which, in turn, created demand for establishing inter-country and intra-country cold-chain networks from farm to the consumers.[1]

In terms of different components of cold-chain, according to the International Association of Refrigerated Warehouses in 2014, the total capacity of refrigerated warehouses worldwide is estimated at 552 million cubic meters, an increase of 92 million cubic meters (20%) over 2012. Countries such as India and China have seen one of the fastest growth in capacity in the recent years.[2] Overall, while developed countries are large and mature markets for cold-chain, developing countries such as India and China are the fastest growing markets, which will provide opportunities for future investment for companies from developed countries who are likely to face a saturated market at home.[3] Figure 2.1 provides a comparative illustration of 20 largest markets in terms of their refrigerated warehousing capacity. India was the second largest in 2010.

India is one of the largest producers of perishable products such as fruits and vegetables, milk and diary, meat and poultry (NCCD, 2014). The consumer base is growing and the purchasing power is rising. This has created the demand for cold-chains. However, the cold-chain infrastructure in India is fragmented and there is a huge wastage of agricultural produce in transportation from farm to the consumers. To minimise the losses, the government is trying to attract private and foreign investment and best practices in cold-chain infrastructure for developments of world-class cold-chain network.

Given this background, the first two sub-sections provide an overview of the cold-chain sector in the UK and India. It provides the present trends and developments in the cold-chain sector, the prevalent regulations and the schemes and incentives offered by the two governments. A primary survey of key stakeholders in the sector has been conducted in India and the UK and the results are summarised in the third sub-section. The last sub-section provides some potential areas of collaborations, case studies and based on this it presents a 'go-to-market' strategy for foreign businesses.

2.1 A Brief Overview of the Sector in the UK

The global market for cold-chains has grown substantially in the recent past and it is projected to reach USD 233,476.7 million by 2019, at a CAGR of 15.6 per cent from 2014 to 2019.[4] In terms of market size, North America garners the largest market share, followed by Europe and then the Asia-Pacific region.

1. See *http://www.igd.com/Research/Supply-chain/Logistics/3457/UK-Food--Grocery-Retail-Logistics-Overview/* (accessed on 3 March 2016).
2. International Association of Refrigerated Warehouses (IARW) (2010).
3. See *http://www.marketsandmarkets.com/Market-Reports/cold-chains-frozen-food-market-811.html* (accessed on 3 March 2016).
4. Obtained from Markets & Markets, November 2014. *http://www.marketsandmarkets.com/Market-Reports/cold-chains-frozen-food-market-811.html* (accessed on 3 March 2016).

Figure 2.1

Capacity of Refrigerated Warehouses in 20 Largest Country Markets (2008 or 2010 as Available) (in Million Cubic Meters)

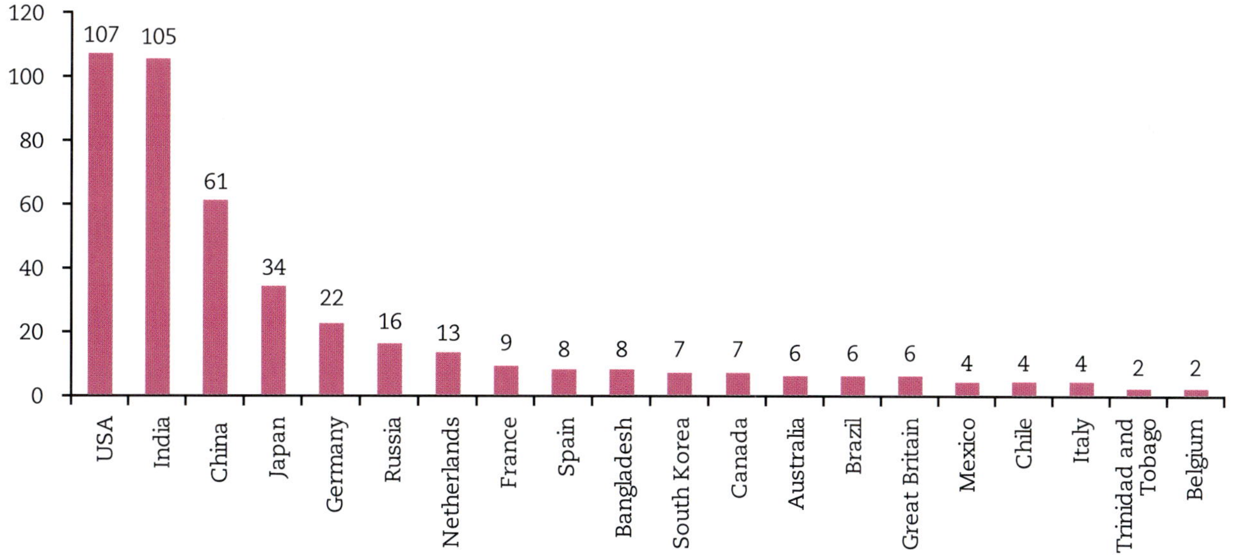

Source: Extracted from International Association of Refrigerated Warehouses (IARW), 2010: 5, Figure 1.

Among developed countries, and particularly in Europe, the UK has one of the leading food supply chain networks. The temperature-controlled logistics market is estimated to be worth about GBP 23 billion (USD 32.6 billion) or 24 per cent of the UK's GBP 96 billion (USD 136.1 billion) road transport market. There were 134,100 temperature-controlled vehicles operating in the UK in 2010.[5]

In terms of regulation, the EU comes up with Directives, which Member States have to follow. This leads to some kind of synergy across regulations of the Member States and help in cross-country movements of fresh and processed products. One such Directive is the EU 'Agreement on the International Carriage of Perishable Foodstuff and on the Special Equipment to be used for such Carriage', which was transposed by the UK in 1980.[6]

The European Food Safety Authority is an autonomous body funded by the EU in order to assess and communicate all risks associated with the complete food chain. In May 2013, the EU published a package of measures, which aims to provide a modernised and simplified approach to strengthen health and safety standards across the agri-chain. Thus, the EU is trying to have a common minimum standard across its Member States so that fresh and chilled products can move smoothly across the EU.

The Food Standards Agency (FSA) is the nodal agency for food safety in the UK while the Department of Transport is responsible for the movement of logistics. In addition, there are industry associations and chambers looking after food logistics supply chain. Among these the Food Storage and Distribution Federation is the key trade body, which represents and supports the interests of the entire food logistics industry in the UK with the purpose of providing support and advice on cost efficiencies, environmental impact and sustainability, good business practice and legislation.

2.2 Overview of the Cold-chain Sector in India

Given the large production and rising consumption, India is facing a growing requirement of cold-chain infrastructure. Though India has large capacity in terms of cold storage infrastructure (see Figure 2.1 and Table 2.2), there are other verticals such as pack-houses, reefer vehicles, etc., where there are significant demand-supply gaps. Hence, there is a scope for attracting investments and improving the cold-chain infrastructure in the country. This sub-section provides an overview of the Indian cold-chain sector giving the industry structure and the trends and developments

5. See *http://naturalleader.com/wp-content/themes/natlead/images/CRC3656-ColdChainOpp.pdf* (accessed on 28 March 2016). Currency conversion is done using *www.oanda.com* (accessed on 29 March 2016) using the exchange rate of GBP 1 = USD1.41.

6. The Agreement on the International Carriage of Perishable Foodstuffs and on the Special Equipment to be used for such Carriage is a 1970 United Nations treaty that establishes standards for the international transport of perishable food between the states that ratify the treaty.

in the sector, the regulatory structure and the schemes and incentives provided by the government.

2.2.1 Industry Structure and Trends and Developments

The Indian cold-chain industry is highly fragmented and around 90 per cent of the companies are in the unorganised or non-corporate sector. Traditionally, cold-chain facilities were used by either the organised dairy industry or fast food chains and QSRs. Most of these businesses invested in establishing their own cold-chain infrastructure. For example, McDonald's invested in cold-chain six years before they entered the Indian market in 1996 (Mukherjee et al., 2014) with the help of Radhakrishna Foodland Private Limited (referred to as RK Foodland). At the same time (around 1993), other global players Snowman Frozen Foods Limited (later changed to Snowman Logistics Limited) entered Indian market.

Since the sector is largely unorganised in nature, there are no clear estimates of the industry size or growth potential. Primary interactions (which will be discussed in the next sub-section) and secondary information reveal that there are more than 3,500 companies present across India,[7] mainly in the private sector, and the sector is dominated by the small and medium enterprises owning less than 5 cold storages or refrigerated vehicles.

A number of agencies have tried to estimate the size of the cold-chain market in India and its future growth potential (See Table 2.1). All these studies project a CAGR in the range of 20-30 per cent. This growth rate in the cold-chain sector has been projected based on economic growth, growth in organised retail, supportive government initiatives, and a shift in taste and preferences, which has fuelled the growth of frozen foods and QSRs.

As mentioned earlier, while India is nearly meeting its cold storage requirement as of now, it faces shortages with respect to other verticals including temperature-control vehicles, pack-houses and ripening chambers (see Table 2.2). The table summarises the status of the Indian cold-chain industry with respect to the current infrastructure (as per recorded data up to March 2014), identifying the gaps.

Looking at the status of various components of cold-chain and the total requirement, it is observed that till date, most of the investments have happened in the cold storage segment. This is because the government incentives have largely focused on development of cold storage infrastructure leading to uneven growth across the different components of cold-chain.

Table 2.1

Selected Studies and Projections

Year	*Reports*	*Period*	*Projection (in percentages)*	*Size & Value (USD billion by 2017)*
Feb. 2013	ASSOCHAM[a]	2015-2020	25.8	10.3
March 2013	NCCD Reefer Conclave[b]	2012-2017	28	11.6
June 2014	Onicra Credit Rating Agency of India Limited[c]	2013-2017	20	10
April 2015	TechNavio[d]	2015-2019	27	N.A.
May 2015	National Cold-chain Summit[e]	2015-2019	28	13

Note: N.A. stands for not available; a: "Cold-chain industry to touch Rs 64,000 cr by 2017: Assocham", *Business Standard*, 17 February 2013. Available at: *http://www.business-standard.com/article/companies/cold-chain-industry-to-touch-rs-64-000-cr-by-2017-assocham-113020600684_1.html* (accessed on 3 March 2016); b. See *http://www.nccd.gov.in/PDF/Report_RTC.pdf* (accessed on 18 August 2015); c. See *http://www.technavio.com/report/cold-chain-logistics-market-in-india-2015-2019* (accessed on 3 March 2016); d. See *http://www.nationalcoldchainsummit.org/ColdChainCurrentScenario.html* (accessed on 3 March 2016); e. See *http://www.onicra.com/images/pdf/publications/coldchainindustryreportjune2014.pdf* (accessed on 3 March 2016).

Source: Compiled by authors from different reports.

Table 2.2

Status of Cold-chain Infrastructure and All India Requirements

Type of Infrastructure	*Current Status*	*All India Requirement*	*Gap*
Cold Storages (bulk and hub)	31,823,700 MT	35,100,662 MT	32,76,962 MT
Temperature-controlled Vehicles	9,000 nos.	61,826 nos.	52,826 nos.
Pack-house	249 nos.	70,080 nos.	69,831 nos.
Ripening Chambers	812 nos.	9,131 nos.	8,319 nos.

Source: NCCD 2015: 16.

As of date, most of the cold-chain players cater to the needs of their clients by collecting the goods from aggregators/large farmers/*mandis* and transporting them to cold storage or processing centres. In very few cases, produce is picked directly from the farm. This is due to lack of pack-houses at the farm level. The NCCD, 2015 study pointed out that India requires 70,080 pack-

7. See *http://indiacoldchainshow.com/Cold-Chain-Industry-in-India-A-Report.pdf* (accessed on 5 October 2015).

houses (see Table 2.2). The study also highlights that bulk of the existing pack-houses are for exports and they are located in a sporadic manner. According to the study, there are 149 operational pack-houses in the country, which are fit for export quality. Overall, the cold-chain is well-developed for exports but not for the domestic market.

India is facing shortage in terms of reefer vehicle capacity with the ratio of reefer vehicles to cold storages is only 1:8. In addition, only 4 million MT of perishable out of the 104 million MT produced, is transported through reefer vehicles. Further, in India around 80 per cent of refrigerated vehicles are dedicated to the transportation of milk; there are only about 9,000 reefer vehicles for the transportation of fresh and processed foods (see Table 2.2). Most of the reefer transport is used for transporting products meant for export. Given the shortage of refrigerated vehicles in India, this is one of the focus areas of the government for future investment.

In terms of products, most of the cold storage facilities in India cater to long-term storage of potatoes, onions and high-value/exports crops such as apples, grapes and flowers. Around 75 per cent of the cold storage capacity is used to store potatoes, while only 23 per cent is available for other perishable produce. Cold storages for meat, fish and dairy items and for other items such as chillies and other spices account for only one per cent of total cold storage capacity. These cold storages are also usually smaller in capacity.

Majority of the multipurpose cold storage capacity are located in the states of Uttar Pradesh, West Bengal, Gujarat, Punjab and Andhra Pradesh. In some states such as Himachal Pradesh, the North East, Tamil Nadu and Odisha, there is severe shortage of cold storage facilities.[8]

In the past, cold storages were built of brick-and-mortar and they were not multi-chambered. As a result, the temperature requirements or humidity levels could not be adjusted to the product requirement. Each product category has different temperature requirement (see Table 2.3).

Cold storages are now constructed to meet product specific requirements and many of them are multi-chambered, which enable storages of different products. Since India continues to suffer from long power cuts, the cold stores are designed to conserve the temperature inside with the help of back-up generators, phase change materials and proper insulation. Also, since India is a net importer of fossil fuel, cold storages are increasingly looking forward to adopting cleaner technologies such as solar energy for electricity generation.

Table 2.3

Selected Commodities and their Desired Storage Conditions

Commodity	*Temperature (F)*	*Relative Humidity (%)*
Apple	30-40	90-95
Grapes	32	85
Bananas	56-58	90-95
Cabbage	32	98-100
Cucumber	50-55	95
Potato	50-60	90

Compiled from: National Sustainable Agriculture Information Service, Postharvest handling of fruits and vegetables available at *https://attra.ncat.org/attra-pub/download.php?id=378* (accessed on 21 August 2015).

The cold-chain industry is mostly demand-led in India. There are at present three types of players operating in the industry.

- First, there are companies such as RK Foodland and ColdEX Logistics Private Limited, which are integrated service providers. The services offered by these players include reefer transportation, providing cold storage infrastructure and other value-added services including sorting, grading and packaging.
- Second, there are companies such as Kelvin Cold-chain Logistics Private Limited and Coldstar Logistics Private Limited that are operating both reefer transportation and cold storage.
- Third, there are players offering standalone services, either in the cold storage or in the reefer transportation. For example, Ice Trail Logistics Private Limited operates only in the reefer transportation services and Blue Star India provides cold storage facilities.

2.2.2 Regulatory Structure

Given the quasi-federal governance structure in India, cold-chains are promoted by both the central and state governments. At the centre, a number of task force and expert committees have been set up to make

8. For details see *http://foodlogistics.in/wp-contentuploads/2016/02/Cold_Chain-_Grid_in_India.pdf* (accessed on 3 March 2016).

Traditional Cold Storage Facilities

Source: http://www.thehindubusinessline.com/economy/agri-business/bengal-hikes-potato-cold-storage-rentals-by-rs-19quintal/article4677242.ece

Source: http://ecoursesonline.iasri.res.in/mod/page/view.php?id=926

Modern Cold Storage

Courtesy: RK Foodland Pvt. Ltd.

policy suggestions regarding the development of cold-chain in India. Based on the recommendations of the Task Force on Development of Cold-chain in India constituted in May 2007 for designing a road map for cold-chains in India, NCCD was established in the year 2012.

NCCD is the nodal agency for cold-chain, which works in close collaboration with multiple government departments including the Ministry of Agriculture, the Ministry of Health and Family Welfare (MoHFW), the Ministry of Road Transport and Highways, the National Horticulture Board with the industry and other stakeholders to promote and develop integrated cold-chain infrastructure in India. NCCD has commissioned a number of studies on the cold-chain sector and is collaborating with industry and international players for the development of the sector. NCCD has also established operational guidelines for cold-chains.

2.2.3 Government Policy and Initiatives for Cold-chain

The development of cold-chain network is one of the key focus areas of the government. Both the central and state governments offer grants, subsidies and tax incentives to the cold-chain sector.

Some of the incentives offered by the central government are given in Box 2.1.[9]

Some of the schemes under which subsidies and grants are offered are given in Table 2.4. In addition, to encourage foreign investment in this sector, the government has allowed 100 per cent FDI through automatic route. A number of state governments help the companies to get concession land through the State Industrial Development Corporations. They also provide benefits such as concession or exemption of stamp duties, reduction in electricity duties through their respective agricultural policies, etc.

2.3 Primary Survey

To understand the experience of cold-chain companies in India, a primary survey of 29 companies has been conducted. The sample includes companies with integrated operations, companies in both warehousing and cold storage, companies operating refrigerated vehicles or cold storages only. It also

9. The box is compiled from the following sources: *http://pib.nic.in/newsite/PrintRelease.aspx?relid=107115; http://103.247.98.218/~mofpi/index.php?option=com_content&view=article&id=320&Itemid=686; http://nccd.gov.in/PDF/Mofpi.pdf; http://nccd.gov.in/PDF/ChallengeColdChain-Development.pdf* (accessed on 3 March 2016).

Box 2.1

Selected Incentives by the Central Government to Cold-chain

- 100 per cent FDI in cold-chains through automatic route.
- Income tax incentives:
  - 100 per cent profit deduction for Income Tax for the first 5 years and 25 per cent for the next 5 years under Section 80-IB.
  - 150 per cent deduction permitted for expenditure incurred on capital investment setting up a cold-chain.
- Custom duty for imports is low or nil:
  - Specified for cold-chain projects at 5 per cent.
  - Reefer vans and containers are nil.
- Service tax exemption for:
  - Storage of agricultural produce in cold storages or warehouses.
  - Erection, installation or commissioning of cold storage equipment, transport, technical testing and analysis service by state or central certification agencies.
  - Services provided by a goods transportation agency for fruits, vegetables, eggs, milk, food grains or pulses.
- Excise duty exemption:
  - For all refrigeration machineries and parts used for installation of cold storage, cold room or refrigerated vehicle.
  - Pasteurising, drying, evaporating, etc. machinery used in dairy sector.

Source: Compiled from various government websites.

covers companies that have received grants for building cold storages under Mega Food Park Scheme of MoFPI.[10] All the companies surveyed are large and mid-sized companies with operations across more than one state.

Majority of the companies surveyed are privately-owned, except the Container Corporation of India (CONCOR), which is a public sector enterprise. CONCOR is present through their subsidiary Fresh and Healthy Enterprise Limited and offers services like pre-cooling, reefer transportation and controlled atmosphere storage. CONCOR is also the sole operator of refrigerated containers through railways since private container train operators are yet to start off for refrigerated container movement. It runs refrigerated containers from ICD in Dadri and ICD Kanpur (both located in the Indian state Uttar Pradesh) to Jawaharlal Nehru Port Trust in Navi Mumbai (Maharashtra) for export of meat.

The survey shows that integrated service providers cater to the requirements of the multinationals primarily including the QSRs, FMCG companies and the retailers. McDonalds has tied up with RK Foodland in India to provide reefer transportation and cold storages, which are essentially doubling as distribution centres across India. Similarly, ColdEX Logistics Private Limited provides a variety of services such as vendor development, market projections, menu development and inventory. This is done at the distribution centres responsible for storing and supplying products to clients such as Burger King. For Burger King, it is the sole distribution partner across India. Kelvin Cold-chain Logistics Private Limited is providing services to many Indian as well as multinational corporations such as Jubilant FoodWorks Limited (Domino's Pizza brand) and Coffee Day Global Limited (Café Coffee Day).

The cold-chain industry in India has been undergoing consolidation through mergers and acquisitions. For example, Gati Limited (which was originally a logistics player), acquired Delhi-based trucking company Kausar India Limited in 2007 to focus primarily on organised retail, food chains, pharmaceutical and dairy industry.

10. This part of the survey was jointly conducted with ICRIER.

Table 2.4

Selected Grant in Aid/Subsidy Provided by the Central Government

Ministry	Scheme Name	Subsidy/Grant	Components	Key Beneficiaries
Ministry of Food Processing Industries	Scheme of Cold-chain, Value Addition and Preservation Infrastructure[1]	Grant-in-aid 50 per cent of the total cost of plant and machinery and technical civil works in general areas (75% for North East region including Sikkim, difficult areas such as J&K, Himachal Pradesh and Uttarakhand) subject to a maximum of INR 100 million (USD 1,491,870)[2]	Pack-houses, ripening chambers, reefer vans, retail outlets, precooling units, primary processing centres, etc.	Individual groups of entrepreneurs, cooperative societies, self-help groups, farmers, producer organisations, non-governmental organisations (NGOs), Central/State PSUs
Ministry of Agriculture	National Horticulture Mission Central government scheme implemented by State Horticulture Missions	Subsidies from 40 to 50 per cent (higher for hilly, scheduled and tribal areas) for different components up to a stipulated amount[3] (see the link in the note for a detailed set up)	Pack-houses, pre-cooling units, mobile pre-cooling units, cold storage and ripening chambers	Fruits and vegetable farmers, aggregators, traders
Ministry of Commerce and Industry (MoCI), Agricultural and Processed Food Products Export Development Authority (APEDA)	Agriculture Export Promotion Plan Scheme: Infrastructure[4] (state governments)	90 per cent grant-in-aid by APEDA and 10 per cent from other government or public sector agency. Other than land, subsidies up to 40 per cent for different components up to a stipulated amount	Pre-coolers, cold storages, specialised storage facilities, pack-houses, processing units.	Exporters
National Horticulture Board (along with National Cooperative Development Corporation)	Commercial Horticulture Scheme[5]	Subsidy of 40 per cent limited to INR 3 million (USD 44,756.1) per project in general areas and 50 per cent of project cost limited to INR 3,750,000 (USD 55,945.1) in North East Region, Hilly and Scheduled areas. Subsidy of 50 per cent limited to INR 5,600,000 (USD 83,544.7) per project as per admissible cost norms for green houses, shade net house, plastic tunnel, anti-bird /hail nets & cost of planting material, etc. Subsidy of 35 per cent limited to INR 5,075,000 (USD 75,712.4) per project in general area and of 50 per cent limited to INR 7,250,000 (USD 108,161) per project in North East, Hilly and Scheduled areas.[6]	Pack-houses, ripening chambers, reefer vans, retail outlets, pre-cooling units, primary processing, etc.	Farmers, entrepreneurs

Source: Different ministry websites. 1. *http://www.mofpi.nic.in/ContentPage.aspx?KYEwmOL+HGpVvrjs+CYNMEVv1Ut2JCKrQBk6eysSpqTcOd6wDMdYMFfszmCLeGQfH3plxGEfuPCI5B/ICcPWtOkuSi8h7TIEgCgbgG2soNfCVKv2q5Y4fA== (accessed on 5 October 2015); 2.* USD 1 = INR 67.03 *(https://www.oanda.com/currency/converter [accessed on March 28 2016); 3. http://nhm.nic.in/Horticulture/Annexure-V.pdf (accessed on 28 March 2016); 4. http://apeda.gov.in/apedawebsite/trade_promotion/Scheme-Component-for-Infrastructure-Development.htm (accessed on 20 August 2015); 5. http://nhb.gov.in/commercial_hort_scheme_guideline.aspx?enc=3ZOO8K5CzcdC/Yq6HcdIxOVZI61DUqgouJqJXNMGIcc= (accessed on 20 August 2015); 6. http://nhb.gov.in/commercial_hort_scheme_guideline.aspx?enc=3ZOO8K5CzcdC/Yq6HcdIxOVZI61DUqgouJqJXNMGIcc (accessed on 28 March 2016).*

To expand their operations, companies are raising funds from different sources. Companies like ColdEX Logistics Private Limited, Snowman Logistics Limited and Gati Kausar India Limited have raised funds in the past through private equity players, public offerings, etc., and they plan to utilise the funds for investing in various components of cold-chain and expanding their operations. For example, in October 2014, Mandala Capital Ltd. (a private equity player focusing exclusively in the food industries sector) invested USD 24.45 million in Gati Kausar India Limited. The company plans to use the funds for building a network of cold storages across the country over the next three years.[11] Snowman Logistics Limited, an integrated player, raised capital through equity shares in the initial public offering.[12] Thus, overall, the companies are trying to integrate and expand their operations.

11. *https://www.gati.com/images/pdf/media-center/press-release/Gati_Ltd_Q2FY15_results.pdf* (accessed on 3 March 2016).

12. *http://www.livemint.com/Money/jefcjrPhOJHXXKuXShwxSM/Snowman-Logistics-shares-jump-70-in-debut-trade.html* (accessed on 3 March 2016).

The survey respondents have provided information of the present status of cold-chain sector, the business model opted by the companies, future growth potential, investment plans, and the use of technology. These findings are given below.

- Status of the cold-chain: A majority of the respondents have mentioned that the cold-chain industry in India is fairly developed for food products including fruits and vegetables, meat and fish that are meant for export. However, as regards the domestic market, the cold-chain industry is still at a very nascent stage. In addition, none of the companies interviewed is sourcing directly from the farmers. This finding is also substantiated by the NCCD, 2015 report. Findings from the primary survey also suggest that setting up of pack-houses, which form an entry point for the cold-chain is the biggest challenge due to several factors such as power problems in villages, land conversion issues, etc., which are discussed in detail in Section 6 highlighting the barriers. They also feel that pack-houses will give maximum benefits to farmers as it serve as a base for pre-cooling, sorting, grading, etc. However, private players are not willing to invest in pack-houses since it is not profitable, and it is difficult to set up the cold-chain transport facilities in villages due to underdeveloped reverse logistics. Farmers, who are users of the cold storage facilities, are often unable to pay the price for the facility.

- Business Model: The business model differs within the cold-chain industry. Most companies operating reefer vehicles either own or lease vehicles. For example, ColdEX Logistics Private Limited owns around 850 reefer trucks, while Snowman Logistics Limited has both owned trucks and leased trucks—it owns around 70-80 reefer trucks and the remaining is hired from other companies. M J Logistics Limited, which is into cold storage business, hires reefer trucks. Kelvin Cold-chain Logistics Private Limited owns fleet of around 200 reefer trucks along with few cold storages across India. Some companies also offer allied services. For instance, Ice Trail Logistics Private Limited offers value-added services like customs clearance services.

In case of reefer transportation, on an average, the running cost per km is around INR 40-60 per kilometre (km) between Delhi and Mumbai for large multi-axle vehicles, which is almost double that of a non-reefer vehicle of similar size. Although the rates that are charged vary across companies and it depends on the capacity of the truck, container size, road conditions and product being transported, among others; in general, the per km charge for a refrigerated vehicle has been found to be almost double the normal vehicle in the same route. The high charges often make it difficult for the farmers and small producers to use the refrigerated vehicles for domestic transportation. Some farmers from Himachal Pradesh have pointed out that it is cheaper for them to transport apples through normal truck in spite of the fact that it may lead to higher wastage. This is due to the fact that while the time taken by both types of vehicle is the same as there are no cold storage facilities in *mandis* outside major cities like Delhi. By contrast, farmers engaged in international trade are willing to pay a higher price because of the lower wastages through refrigerated vehicles and higher realisation in prices. Also, the refrigerated transport facility ensures quality which is needed for exports.

Similarly, the cost of a pallet in cold storage is higher than the cost of storage in normal warehouses. The survey has found that cold storage providers charge anywhere between INR 1,200-2,000 per pallet/month. The charges depend on the palette rental, type of cold storage and any value-added services, if offered. A leading Indian retailer, looking at the increased demand for processed food in India, recently came up with an MFP in southern state of India. It offered cold storage, individual quick freezing (IQF) freezers and deep freezer facilities at MFP. Total cold storage capacity is 660 MT while IQF and deep freezer capacity is 1000 MT. Other value-added services on offer include pack-house wherein it is offering washing, sorting, grading and packaging facilities. Table 2.5 presents the rentals, as being charged by the MFP developer, which help develop a cold storage with grant from the MoFPI. Overall, the rental for the cold-chain is high which makes it unattractive to users such as farmers for domestic market.

- Future Growth: The survey respondents have pointed out that the expected growth rate of the cold-chain sector is likely to be in double digits, while certain respondents have mentioned that the sector is likely to grow at the rate of 20 per cent over the next five years owing to increased investments, modernisation of existing facilities, and establishments of new ventures through private and government partnerships. The growth of the sector is driven by the growth of the Indian economy, which they expect to be in a high growth trajectory for the next five years. Low interest rates and corporate taxes rather than government grants and subsidies according to survey respondents will drive the future growth of this sector.

Table 2.5

Rentals Charged by the Mega Food Park Developer

Services	*Charges*
Cold Rooms/Storage	INR 2050/pallet/month
Freezer Rooms	INR 2500/pallet/month
Spiral Freezer for Readt to Eat Food	INR 8/kg of output
Grading & Sorting of Fruits & Vegetables (value-added services)	INR 1/kg of output

Source: ICRIER and Dun and Bradstreet Tangram Survey of Mega Food Parks.

- Investment Plan: The survey also shows that companies investing in the cold-chain sector should plan for long-term investment. The break-even period for investment is 8-9 years. Hence, businesses have to plan their investment accordingly and access to finance with lower interest rates is required by businesses. The survey also points out that companies need economies of scale and the businesses are willing to make investment to reap the benefits of economies of scale given a stable political and economic scenario. However, the government should provide them the conducive investment environment by reducing barriers identified in Section 6.

During the survey, it is noticed that a lot of companies are planning to expand their operations to provide complete end-to-end solutions to their clients. For example, Gati Kausar India Limited that currently operates only in the reefer transportation services is planning to enter into cold storage business. Similarly, M J Logistics Services Limited, currently in cold storage space, is planning to enter reefer transportation segment and plans to buy around 9-10 reefer vehicles. ColdEX Logistics Private Limited, which is an integrated cold-chain player, is planning to expand cold storage facilities across 8 locations in India, covering mainly large cities. Majority of the respondents have been able to raise funds from the market for their planned expansion.

- Technology: The available technology and requirement of technology vary with the type of players and their segment of operation.

- Reefer transportation: It has three major components—truck chassis, container/box and the refrigeration equipment. During the survey, most of the transportation players have mentioned that they use standard chassis manufactured by Indian companies including Tata Motors (Tata Group), Ashok Leyland (Hinduja Group), Eicher Motors (Eicher Group). In some cases, chassis have been procured from global players including MAN Trucks and Hino Trucks (Toyota Group). A majority of the companies use trucks manufactured in India and hardly anyone uses the imported truck chassis. In certain cases, for instance, long hauls, foreign brands, namely MAN Trucks and Hino Trucks, are preferred.

Most of the companies redesign the vehicles as per their requirements. For this they either procure refrigerated units, containers, etc., from companies present in India such as Thermo King Corporation (refrigeration provider), Carrier Corporation (refrigeration provider), HLM India Private Limited (reefer box manufacturer) or import directly from the foreign manufacturer. In certain cases, boxes/containers are imported from European countries, namely Germany and the Netherlands and, in some cases, Middle Eastern countries such as Kuwait. Imported containers, especially from the Netherlands and Germany, which are considered to be the best in quality as they have the ability to handle multiple temperatures. Their weight is also lighter than the Indian-made containers. Indian respondents are not aware of the available technologies in the UK and none of the UK companies is found to be present in this segment.

In the refrigeration segment, there are two major global equipment manufacturers in India, namely Thermo King Corporation and Carrier Corporation of USA. Other players offering refrigeration equipment includes Hwa-Sung of Korea. No Indian and UK brand is found to be present in this segment during the survey.

- Cold storage technology—During the survey, it has emerged that there are two types of cold storages operational in India—the storages using old technology and those using modern technology. The cold storages that use the state-of-art technology are generally multi-chambered and multi-temperature controlled with multiple racks. Compared to this, the cold storages using old technology are air conditioned brick-and-mortar buildings and are mostly used for storing potatoes. In such a case, it is possible to control only the temperature but not the humidity.

- Alternate sources of technology: A number of respondents have highlighted the need for alternate clean technologies in the cold-chain industry such as solar energy to run the cold storage or pack-houses and electric powered reefer trucks. In the villages, there is shortage of power and solar energy can be an alternative and clean source of energy for the pack-houses and cold storages. Fuel efficient trucks will also help reduce pollutions. However, renewable technology is costly in India. There is a need to make clean technology financially and commercially viable. The survey participants have pointed out that, even in the UK, companies are trying to make clean technology commercially viable. The concept of battery operated truck is coming up. However, that would need battery charging stations along with fuel refuelling stations. Respondents feel that some of the new technologies can be tried along the economic corridors such as DMIC. The respondents further feel that in India the fuel cost is high due to heavy containers. There is scope for introducing light weight containers in reefer transportation. This will help reduce the overall weight of the vehicle and will provide better fuel efficiency.

2.4 Opportunities and Go-to-Market Strategy for the UK Companies

The above analysis reflects that while there is scope for investments in cold-chain in India, at present, the presence of companies from the UK in the country is limited. Unlike the companies from the UK, there are investments from other European countries such as the Netherlands and Germany. Thus, the UK businesses are somewhat late in entering the Indian market. The survey also shows that there is potential for investment from the UK in the cold-chain sector. Some of these are listed below:

- Provide alternate and clean sources of energy: At present, the energy costs including fuel and power costs in India are high. This is adversely affecting the financial viability of the cold-chain industry. Moreover, the entire cold-chain industry is dependent on power from the grid or from sources such as standalone diesel-run gensets. The UK companies can introduce energy saving processes and cleaner and greener technologies like solar powered pack-houses and cold storages. This will ensure the use of renewable source of energy in the industry.

  It is found during the survey that Dearman Technologies, a UK-based company, plans to roll out clean cold technology in India to move perishable goods efficiently from producer to consumer. Other UK companies can also explore the Indian market.

- Supply containers and other parts: As mentioned in the previous section, the survey respondents have pointed out that containers made in India are bulkier and heavier than the containers from European countries and other developed parts of the world. As a result, containers from Germany, the Netherlands, etc., are imported by the cold-chain players. Till date, the presence of UK companies in this area has been limited. The UK companies can export or manufacture light weight containers in India, which will ensure better fuel efficiency.

- Set up state-of-the art services stations along highway: The UK companies can work with the Indian government to set up state-of-the-art service stations for trucks that have charging facilities and rest area for drivers in the industrial corridors such as DMIC. The amenities offered in these refuelling stations can include cheap overnight accommodations for drivers and amenities like clean public toilets, canteens or food courts, rest rooms, truck washing facilities and truck repair services, among others.

- Provide consultancy and training services for integrated cold-chain development: Given its proven competence in development of cold-chains from farm-to-fork, the UK companies can offer consultancy and training services to Indian companies in establishing cold-chains from farm-to-fork. One of the key issues faced by trucking companies is reverse logistics. In this area,the UK companies can help set up the logistics network. The UK companies can also offer consultancy services and training in areas related to product handling in cold-chain and in maintaining food safety standards and clean technologies.

As mentioned in the previous section, the UK companies can enter India as a 100 per cent wholly owned subsidiary or through a joint venture with an Indian partner. Foreign investors that are bringing in new technology are encouraged in the country. This sector has huge scope for technology transfer. Foreign companies can establish manufacturing presence in India, particularly, with respect to manufacturing of equipment related to the cold-chain sector.

India is not a homogeneous market. Different states have different operating environment and therefore, the businesses have to be careful while choosing their states for operations. While cold storages, etc., can be located closer to the main production and consumption centres, the companies can set up service stations and charging stations along the economic and industrial corridors. Further, it may be more financially viable for companies to start operations around the national highways and economic corridors where the infrastructure for logistics service providers is good.

The UK companies in cold storages and reefer vehicles should choose states with good agricultural productions and agro-processing facilities. The UK equipment manufacturing companies can select states that provide ease of doing business and congenial manufacturing environment and good infrastructure. They also should do market feasibility study and try to identify some customers/users of the cold-chain infrastructure. It is also worth mentioning that India is a price sensitive market and the UK companies should have the competitive prices for products and services. The UK companies should be aware of their competitors, including their competitors from the EU Member States, and know the strength of their competitors. The UK companies should also evaluate the incentives given by the central and state governments and understand how they can dovetail the benefits.

Companies may face some difficulties in doing business across states. The Indian central and state governments are trying to attract investment in newly created states such as the state of Andhra Pradesh and in the hilly regions such as the North East. The north-east and eastern part of India will be linked to the Association of Southeast Asian Nations (ASEAN) countries in the future and the UK companies should explore opportunities in these states.

Entry of UK businesses can be supported by UKTI and UKIBC. UKTI and UKIBC can help by conducting seminars and events on regular basis, which will facilitate business-to-business interactions. It can work closely with Indian government bodies such as NCCD on training programme, R&D, etc. In such events, the UK companies can showcase their latest technologies and services, which can be adopted by India. UKTI and UKIBC can regularly interact with state governments such as the state governments of Maharashtra and Andhra Pradesh who are keen on creating agricultural infrastructure. Joint events with the state government agriculture departments will enable the UK companies to know the state policies and also they can meet potential partners.

These initiatives will aid the UK and Indian businesses to collaborate in establishing a cold-chain network in India, which will benefit the Indian food businesses and the UK companies likewise.

Section 3

Packaging Technology in Food Business

> Packaging is defined as a coordinated system of preparing goods for transport, distribution, storage, retailing and end use, a means of ensuring safe delivery to the ultimate consumer in sound condition at optimum cost and a techno-commercial function aimed at optimizing the costs of delivery while maximizing sales (Coles and Kirwan 2011: 9).

Packaging can broadly be classified into primary packaging, secondary packaging and tertiary packaging. Primary packaging involves immediate packaging of any commodity. For example, plastic wrapping, cans and bottles. Secondary packaging is the additional packaging usually surrounding the primary packaging. Cartons used for keeping packets of a product are an example of secondary packaging. Tertiary packaging is the outermost layer containing several secondary packages. It facilitates warehousing, shipping, etc. Packaging serves four purposes, namely containment, protection, convenience and communication (for details see Robertson, 2012).

Food packaging is the most complex segment of packaging sector, which involves use of sophisticated machines and techniques to help increase the shelf life of products, ensure food safety and quality and reduce wastage. Food packaging is a key component of the food supply chain as the volume and density of packages determine storage as well as transport costs of a food product. At the farm end of the supply chain, collection is affected by the available packaging technology. At the consumer end of the supply chain, packaging determines the ergonomics and aesthetics of a food product. Increasing food safety awareness and changing consumer preferences increase the need for better packaging methods.

In developed countries such as the UK, modern forms of packaging technology such as modified atmosphere packaging, aseptic packaging, etc., are used widely which help reduce the food wastage in supply chain. The UK food packaging industry is highly sophisticated, using modern technologies. Innovation is the key driver of growth. However, the UK food market is becoming saturated and the growth of the food industry is slowing down. This can adversely affect the food packaging sector. By contrast, Indian food market is growing at a fast pace and the food packaging industry although at the nascent stage, is growing at a fast pace. In India, there are substantial losses in the food supply chain due to the use of traditional methods of packaging and low levels of sophistication in food packaging technology. Also, in recent years, there have been concerns about consumer safety in food products and there is increased emphasis on food packaging technology in ensuring consumer safety and health[1]. Given this background, there is scope for mutually beneficial collaboration, technology inflow and investment from the UK companies in the packaging sector in India. This section highlights the possibilities of trade, investment and collaboration between India and the UK.

The layout of this section is as follows: sub-section 3.1 discusses the status of packaging industry globally, in the UK and India based on secondary literature. Sub-section 3.2 examines the governance structure, regulatory framework of the Indian packaging industry and government initiatives and schemes for the packaging sector. Sub-section 3.3 examines the status of packaging technology industry in India and the UK based on a primary survey of industry associations, packaging companies and policymakers in India and the UK. Based on the findings of the primary survey, the last sub-section highlights areas of cooperation and collaboration between India and the UK and provides a go-to-market strategy for the UK companies.

3.1 Overview of Packaging Industry

Global consumer packaging market was valued at USD 400 billion in 2012 (Ernst & Young, 2013). The EU is a major player in packaging industry (Figure 3.1) and Brazil, Russia, India and China comprise approximately 30 per cent of the global demand for packaging.[2]

Figure 3.1

Global Packaging Industry in 2012 (in per cent)

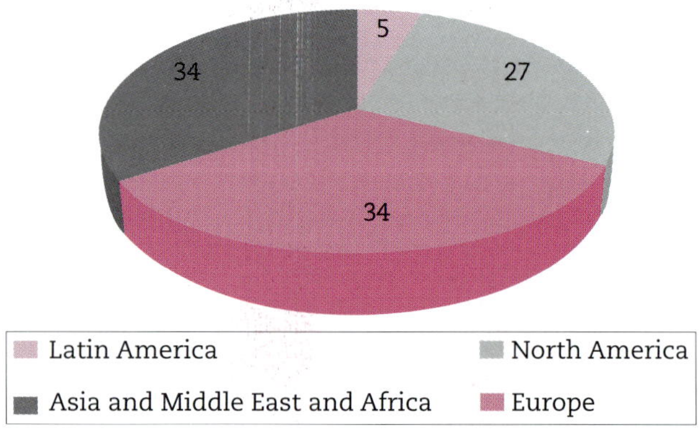

Source: Extracted from Ernst & Young (2013: 2, Chart 1).

1. *http://www.printweek.in/Feature/400375,safety-of-food-under-scanner.aspx* (accessed on 14 March 2016).
2. *http://www.ey.com/Publication/vwLUAssets/Unwrapping_the_packaging_industry_%E2%80%93_seven_factors_for_success/$FILE/EY_Unwrapping_the_packaging_industry_-_seven_success_factors.pdf* (accessed on 11 March 2016).

Food packaging comprised 51 per cent of the global packaging market in 2012. It is projected to grow at a rate of 3.4 per cent on average and reach USD 284 billion by 2018 (Smithers Pira, 2013). The global food packaging machinery market was valued at USD 33.4 billion in 2013 and is expected grow at a 4.6 per cent annual rate through 2017 to USD 41.8 billion.[3]

Existing studies highlight that there have been continuous innovations and developments in food packaging. For example, innovations such as active packaging and intelligent packaging have helped increase shelf life of food products. Among active technologies, oxygen scavenger, moisture absorbers and barrier packaging represented more than 80 per cent of the active technologies market in 2008[4]. Green packaging is another recent development. The global green packaging market was USD 132.47 billion in 2014 and it is expected to grow to USD 203.15 billion by 2021. Food and beverage segment accounts for the highest market share (59.7%) in the green packaging market.[5]

The focus on cost reduction has increased the scope of flexible packaging. It is a fast growing segment in the global food packaging industry with a wide variety of cheap plastics being developed. The market tonnage in this segment was around 24.3 million tonnes in 2013 and is forecasted to grow at a CAGR of 4.1 per cent during the period 2013-2018, to reach a total of 29.8 million tonnes. Asia-Pacific has the largest regional flexible market size occupying a share of almost 38 per cent of global market volume, and is predicted to be the fastest growing market for consumer flexible packaging in the period 2013-2018.[6]

3.1.1 Overview of Packaging Industry in the UK

In 2010, the UK packaging industry was valued at around USD 20 billion, 70 per cent of which was consumed by the food and beverage industry.[7] The packaging manufacturing industry has annual sales of over GBP 11 billion (USD 15.6 billion)[8] and employs around 85,000 people. Modern packaging technology in the UK has enabled food wastages in the supply chain to be as low as 3 per cent.[9]

According to a study by PCI Films Consulting Limited, the UK's flexible packaging market was valued at around EUR 1.5 billion (USD 1.65 billion)[10] in 2013, accounting for around 12 per cent of the total European market for flexible packaging.[11] Companies in the UK such as Tesco Plc have been engaged in innovations in active packaging technologies for food packaging. The UK also has several eco-friendly packaging companies such as London Bio Packaging Limited and Biopac UK Limited that provide biodegradable disposables and packaging items reducing the environmental damage by replacing oil-based and other unsustainable materials.

There are niche players in different types of packaging. For example, some of the major players in the UK in plastic packaging industry include LINPAC Group Limited, RPC Group Plc. and APPE Plc.

Overall, the UK packaging market is highly developed and is led by private players. The government plays the role of a facilitator, and the policy focus is on food safety standards. FSA is the regulatory body responsible for food safety and hygiene. The national packaging regulations broadly cover basic requirements of packaging and optimal packaging waste management. The two important national legislations in place are The Packaging (Essential Requirements) Regulations 2015[12] and The Producer Responsibility Obligations (Packaging Waste) Regulations 2007.[13] The Packaging (Essential Requirements) Regulations 2015 specify the rules for concentration levels of regulated metals present in packaging, define the enforcement authority and specify the offences and penalties, among others.

3. *http://www.freedoniagroup.com/industry-study/3063/world-packaging-machinery.htm* (accessed on 11 March 2016).
4. *http://www.innoresearch.net/report_summary.aspx?id=68&pg=107&rcd=FT-102&pd=7/1/2009* (accessed on 11 March 2016).
5. *http://www.transparencymarketresearch.com/pressrelease/green-packaging-market.htm* (accessed on 11 March 2016).
6. *http://www.smitherspira.com/news/2013/october/global-flexible-packaging-industry-growth-to-2018* (accessed on 11 March 2016).
7. *http://www.packaging-gateway.com/features/featureunited-kingdom-packaging-industry-forecast-until-2015/* (accessed on 11 March 2016).
8. Currency conversion is done using *www.oanda.com* (accessed on 29 March 2016) using the exchange rate of GBP 1 = USD 1.41.
9. *http://www.packagingfedn.co.uk/images/reports/The%20UK%20Packaging%20Manufacturing%20Industry%20-%20A%20Brief%20for%20MP's%20&%20Peers%20-%20June%202012.pdf* (accessed on 11 March 2016).
10. Converted using Oanda currency converter. *http://www.oanda.com/currency/converter/* (Exchange rate: EUR 1=USD 1.1 as on 11 March 2016).
11. *http://www.packagingnews.co.uk/features/packaging-in-2015/flexible-07-01-2015* (accessed on 11 March 2016).
12. *http://www.legislation.gov.uk/uksi/2015/1640/pdfs/uksi_20151640_en.pdf* (accessed on 11 March 2016).
13. *http://www.legislation.gov.uk/uksi/2007/871/pdfs/uksi_20070871_en.pdf* (accessed on 11 March 2016).

The Producer Responsibility Obligations (Packaging Waste) Regulations 2007 specify the recovery and recycling obligations for producers. It sets obligation upon the producers in order for the UK to attain the recovery and recycling targets set out in Article 6(1) of Council Directive 94/62/EC of the EU on packaging and packaging waste.

3.1.2 Overview of Packaging Industry in India

The packaging sector is one of the fast growing sectors in India. In the years 2008-2012, the industry grew at about 13.7 per cent (Aranca, 2012). From being the twelfth largest packaging industry in 2009, India became the sixth largest market in 2011 with annual sales of USD 24.6 billion and it is expected to become the fourth largest market in 2016 with annual sales of USD 43.7 billion.[14] It is projected that the Indian packaging industry is expected to grow at 15 per cent per annum with flexible packaging growing at 17 per cent per annum and rigid packaging growing at 14 per cent per annum in the period 2013-2018 [Federation of Indian Chambers of Commerce and Industry (FICCI), 2014]. Flexible packaging industry is one of the fastest growing industries within Indian packaging industry. It was valued at INR 135 billion in 2012.[15]

Processed food packaging is the largest component of the Indian packaging market, followed by personal care packaging (Figure 3.2). Around 40 large players account for about 70 per cent of the total market (Aranca, 2012). There are around 22,000 registered packaging companies in India, more than 85 per cent of which are micro, small and medium enterprises (MSMEs) [Centre for Market Research & Social Development (CMSD), 2013]. In the packaging machinery segment, there are over 600 packaging machinery manufacturers in India, 95 per cent of which are SMEs.[16]

In terms of location, food packaging industry is found in MSME clusters around India. The main clusters of food packaging industry are present in the states of Bihar, Andhra Pradesh, Madhya Pradesh, Chhattisgarh, Gujarat and Maharashtra (CMSD, 2013). Packaging material industry is also found in clusters. Some of the major clusters are paper-based packaging cluster in Parwanoo (Himachal Pradesh), printing and packaging cluster in Ludhiana (Punjab) and plastic packaging cluster in Gautam Buddha Nagar (Uttar Pradesh).

Figure 3.2

Indian Packaging Industry: Sector-wise Breakup (in per cent)

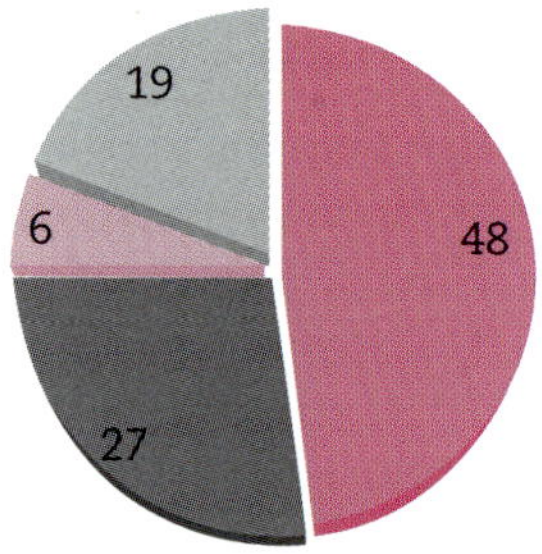

Source: Extracted from CMSD (2013, chart 1). Available at: *http://www.nsic.o.in/study/techgapstudy.pdf* (accessed on 11 March 2016).

Although modern technologies like aseptic packaging and intelligent packaging have been introduced in India, they are yet to be adopted on a larger scale. Table 3.1 shows the major technologies used by MSMEs in India for various food products vis-à-vis countries such as the UK.

Table 3.1

Food Packaging Technology Adopted by MSMEs

Food Segment	Technology (majorly adopted by MSMEs)	International Trend
Raw Food	Pouch Packaging	Vacuum Packaging
	Heat Seal Packaging	Freeze-Thaw Dehydration
	Manual Packaging	Freeze-Thaw Dehydration
Processed	Pouch Packaging	Tetra Pack
	Aseptic Packaging	Aseptic Packaging
	Vacuum Packaging	Injection Moulded Plastic Container Packaging
	Heat Seal Packing	Inert Gas packaging
Semi-Processed	Vacuum Packaging	Vacuum Packaging
	Pouch Packaging	Tetra Packaging
	Aseptic Packaging	Aseptic Packaging
	Heat Seal Packaging	Skin Packaging

Source: Extracted from CMSD (2013: 73). Available at *http://www.nsic.co.in/study/techgapstudy.pdf* (accessed on 15 March 2016).

Table 3.1 highlights that India needs to improve the technology used in packaging industry and match it

14. *http://www.researchandmarkets.com/reports/2000951/packaging_industry_outlook_in_india_market_size* (accessed on 11 March 2016).
15. *http://www.consultmcg.com/blog/the-market-for-flexible-packaging-in-india-for-consumer-markets/* (accessed on 11 March 2016).
16. *http://www.indiapackagingshow.com/industry.htm* (accessed on 11 March 2016).

with global technologies in food packaging. In this context, it is worth noting that packaging is a sector where the Indian government is encouraging foreign investment and a number of foreign companies are present in India. Figure 3.3 shows select foreign players in the Indian packaging industry and their segment of operations.

3.2 India's Trade in Packaging Machinery and Raw Materials

Raw materials and machinery are two important components of packaging. With the modern forms of packaging being developed, the role of sophisticated machinery has increased in food packaging while

Figure 3.3

Select Foreign Players in Indian Packaging Industry

Huhtamaki PPL Limited (Finland)	*Amcor Flexibles India Private Limited* (Australia)	*Bell Packaging India Private Limited* (UK)	*Bosch Limited* (Germany)	*Bossar Packaging Private Limited* (Spain)
Flexible Packaging (including food)	Processed food packaging	Packaging solutions in PVC (Polyvinyl chloride), PET (Polyethylene terepthalate) and PP (Polypropylene)	Packaging machinery for food and pharmaceutical packaging	R&D in packaging technology
Labelling Technologies	Packaging material manufacturing including films, foils and laminates	Prototype and sampling facility		Packaging machinery for food, beverages and pharmaceutical products

Note: Countries in bracket are the respective countries of origin of the companies.
Source: Compiled from the websites of the companies.

Table 3.2

India's Trade in Select Packaging Machinery and Material (in USD '000)

Category	*Flow*	*2009*	*2010*	*2011*	*2012*	*2013*	*2014*
India's Global Trade							
Plates, sheets, film, foil & strip, of polymers of vinyl chloride (HS code 392049)	Export	22007.72	30227.62	38188.29	49491.88	41668.58	44583.07
	Import	81219.22	68179.6	70489.3	73652.72	65041.5	71851.32
Articles for conveyance and packaging of goods, of plastics (HS code 392390)	Export	35124.64	45646.57	86397.57	85136.4	90342.36	76352.04
	Import	32293.12	40966.94	44196.7	49103.7	58998.23	66821.06
Packing containers of paper/paperboard/cellulose wadding/webs of cellulose fibres (HS code 481950)	Export	4112.234	5926.572	8597.915	9576.107	9635.858	8178.888
	Import	4076.724	7172.981	5722.616	5887.242	9385.406	11439.07
Aluminium foil, whether/not printed, not backed, of a thickness not greater than 0.2mm (HS code 760719)	Export	21778.44	28067.06	28894.05	32883.04	42288.1	40909.96
	Import	58051.06	73549.74	126077.5	102627.1	118816	118874.1
Packing/wrapping machinery, including heat-shrink wrapping machinery (HS code 842240)	Export	18426.8	23317.56	34590.41	34233.28	45850.83	31235.19
	Import	80400.37	91760.62	172418.8	146258.1	162437.7	114934.6
Parts of dish-washing machines, packing or wrapping machinery and other machinery (HS code 842290)	Export	17383.54	19322.22	26522.45	27320.42	35727.38	43434.87
	Import	43663.91	46339.85	70555.83	87523.38	83404.96	58428.81
India-UK Trade							
Plates, sheets, film, foil & strip, of polymers of vinyl chloride (HS code 392049)	Export	76.18	439.644	2191.684	4096.602	331.465	236.677
	Import	166.078	388.826	229.631	408.699	341.283	270.269
Articles for conveyance and packaging of goods, of plastics (HS code 392390)	Export	4715.688	6096.301	9707.196	9561.795	6977.709	6251.097
	Import	492.729	751.552	816.25	907.136	797.856	5323.641
Packing containers of paper/paperboard/cellulose wadding/webs of cellulose fibres (HS code 481950)	Export	219.123	1045.763	1440.047	913.155	823.594	914.044
	Import	38.829	36.98	55.725	56.061	82.286	170.482
Aluminium foil, whether/not printed, not backed, of a thickness not greater than 0.2mm (HS code 760719)	Export	640.22	391.344	228.473	303.734	1150.564	881.372
	Import	2027.647	453.104	614.064	255.723	32.384	12.697
Packing/wrapping machinery, including heat-shrink wrapping machinery (HS code 842240)	Export	291.714	448.492	1182.824	120.844	884.436	1106.824
	Import	1098.103	2002.344	9894.637	6794.778	4828.044	3686.593
Parts of dish-washing machines, packing or wrapping machinery and other machinery (HS code 842290)	Export	1077.53	1295.352	1529.317	1857.13	2434.712	2124.468
	Import	461.743	1726.043	6025.931	4921.523	1161.048	581.864

Source: Extracted from World Integrated Trade Solution Database; *http://wits.worldbank.org/* (accessed on 16 March 2016).

innovations in raw materials have resulted in lowering the cost of packaging and reducing the carbon footprint of packaging materials.

This section discusses India's trade in raw materials and packaging machinery. While some of the raw materials are domestically sourced, others are imported. Most of the sophisticated high-end machineries are imported but companies in India also manufacture and export machinery. Table 3.2 shows India's trade patterns with the world and the UK in select raw materials which are used by packaging industry and packaging machinery.

In case of raw materials, India is a net importer of plates, sheets, film, foil and strip, of polymers of vinyl chloride that are used for food packaging, while for articles used for conveyance and packaging made of plastics, India is a net exporter with the world. Overall, India's trade in packaging raw materials with the UK as a share of India's global trade was less than 4 per cent during the period 2009-2014.

In the case of packaging machinery and parts of packaging machinery, India is a net importer with the world. India's trade with the UK in packaging machinery and parts of packaging machinery as a share of its total trade was around 3.7 per cent during the period 2009-2014. Although the volume of trade in packaging machinery with the UK is low, unlike its global trade pattern where the country is a net importer, India is net exporter of parts of packing or wrapping machinery and other machinery and apparatus related to packaging machinery to the UK.

3.3 Governance Structure, Incentives and Regulation

Packaging industry falls under the purview of multiple ministries. For example, plastics manufacturing is governed by the Ministry of Chemicals and Petrochemicals, whereas the food safety aspects of packaging fall under the purview of Food Safety and Standards Authority of India (FSSAI), under MoHFW. To support the packaging industry, the Ministry of Commerce and Industry (MoCI) has also established the Indian Institute of Packaging (IIP), a national apex body for packaging research and training. IIP provides testing facilities to the industry for domestic distribution and export as per national and international standards like Bureau of Indian Standards (BIS), ISO and British Standards, among others. R&D activities pursued by IIP enhance packaging technologies for various food products.[17]

Food processing sector is a priority sector eligible for certain incentives of the Indian government. Packaging is an allied industry and it can reap the benefits of such incentives. FDI up to 100 per cent is allowed in manufacturing and the government is trying to attract foreign investments through various schemes and initiatives such as 'Make in India'. Further, in the Union Budget of 2016-17, it has been proposed that up to 100 per cent FDI will be allowed through the FIPB route in marketing of food products produced and manufactured in India. This is likely to give a boost to the food packaging industry.

To promote manufacturing, the government has adopted a cluster-based approach to manufacturing—packaging companies can avail benefits under schemes such as the Scheme for Setting up Plastic Parks of the Ministry of Chemicals and Petrochemicals[18] and Mega Food Park Scheme of MoFPI.[19] However, most of the benefits are given to the cluster developers under such schemes.

The National Mission on Food Processing supports research proposals for development of innovative products, processes and improvement in manufacturing practices that lead to enhancement of quality and shelf life of food products. More recently, the government came up with the 'Start-up India' scheme that provides direct tax benefits to new and innovative businesses.

The excise duties on raw materials and machinery imports have been reduced overtime. For example, in the Union Budget 2014-15, Indian government, in order to scale up the processing capacity, reduced excise duty on specified food processing and packaging machinery from 10 per cent to 6 per cent.

In terms of regulation, FSSAI, under the aegis of MoHFW is responsible for setting the standards and regulations for food packaging. Food Safety and Standards (Packaging and Labelling) Regulations, 2011[20] provide a detailed account of the different packaging and labelling requirements to be fulfilled for different food products. Chapter 2 of the Food Safety and Standards (Packaging and labelling) Regulations, 2011 specifies different packaging requirements for different

17. For details, see *http://www.iip-in.com/site/default.aspx* (accessed on 11 March 2016).

18. *http://chemicals.nic.in/sites/default/files/FPP260613.pdf* (accessed on 11 March 2016).

19. For details, see *http://mofpi.nic.in* /(accessed on 15 March 2016).

20. For details, see *http://www.fssai.gov.in/Portals/0/Pdf/Food%20Safety%20and%20standards%20(Packaging%20and%20Labelling)%20regulation,%202011.pdf* (accessed on 15 March 2016).

materials and labelling requirements. It provides guidelines for metal containers, containers made of plastic materials, packaging specific requirements for milk and milk products and packaging requirements for drinking water. Labelling requirements specify that a declaration on a package should be made in either English or Hindi. They provide the basic disclosure requirements which include the name of the food product, list of ingredients and nutritional information.

Legal Metrology Act, 2009[21] establishes uniform standards of weights and measures for food packaging. It mandates the disclosure of net quantity of a pre-packaged commodity in accordance with standard unit weight, measure or numeration. It also specifies the penalty on selling of non-standard packages. Apart from these regulations, Environmental Protection Act, 1986[22] and Plastic Waste (Management and Handling) Rules, 2011[23] provide environmental standards for packaging and specify prohibitive activities.

3.4 Primary Survey

To examine the growth drivers of this sector and the potential areas of opportunity for the foreign businesses in the Indian packaging industry, a primary survey has been conducted. The survey covers 31 stakeholders including industry associations, packaging companies, MFPs and policymakers in India and the UK. Survey respondents from India are asked to describe their business model and operations, technology used, identify the technological gaps, identify areas for collaborations with the UK companies in the Indian packaging industry, among others. Respondents from the UK are asked to describe their major strengths in packaging technology, their interest in entering Indian markets, how they identify their partners, and their concerns about entering Indian markets, their views on collaborations and joint partnerships, among others.

Overall the survey shows that a major difference in the food supply chain between India and the UK is that food wastage in the UK is at the consumer end whereas in India it is mainly within the food supply chain due to the lack of modern supply chain infrastructure, handling and packaging technologies. Hardly any UK companies have presence in India. Some of the key findings of the survey in the UK are presented below followed by the key findings of the survey in India.

The UK Survey: The survey shows that the packaging industry in the UK is dominated by large players and many of them are multinational companies. The industry also has small players that rely on innovative practices to compete with the bigger global and regional players. Within the packaging industry in the UK, plastics industry is the most diverse in terms of products and innovation.

The survey participants have pointed out that packaging technologies used in the UK are geared to modern supply chain, storage and handling procedures. These may not be directly replicated in India. In India, packaging companies have to customise their technologies and processes keeping in mind the fragmented nature of supply chain, varied climatic condition, lack of storage facilities, high incidence of spoilage, etc. This requires market knowledge and understanding and at present their knowledge about the Indian market is low.

When asked about the scope for collaboration, the UK companies have pointed out that there is scope for them to collaborate with Indian companies in packaging segment as the food supply chain in India is getting modernised and there is entry of corporate players in manufacturing and food retailing. The shift in consumer food habits to packaged food will also create opportunities for investment in India. However, they would like to enter the market with some of their existing retail and manufacturing partners. The survey shows that the UK companies tend to first expand their presence in the domestic market and then in the EU and then to other markets. They also follow their business partners—the manufacturers and retailers in market expansion. Thus, most of the UK packaging companies will come to India when the UK retailers and manufacturers enter the market.

While the UK companies are willing to expand their operations and enter new markets such as India, they are facing some issues in their domestic market. The UK market is going through a food deflation and there is a slowdown in demand for processed food. Further, there are political and business uncertainties. The companies are waiting for the referendum in the UK to be held on 23 June 2016 that concerns the decision of the UK to be a part of the EU. The referendum has created business uncertainty and can impact the trade and investment decisions of the UK companies, including packaging companies. If the UK decides to

21. For details, see *http://consumeraffairs.nic.in/consumer/sites/default/files/userfiles/LM-Notification09.pdf* (accessed on 15 March 2016).
22. For details, see *http://envfor.nic.in/legis/env/env1.html* (accessed on 15 March 2016).
23. For details, see *http://www.moef.nic.in/downloads/public-information/DOC070211-005.pdf* (accessed on 16 March 2016).

come out of the EU, it will have an implication on the companies sourcing decisions as they will no longer benefit from the EU trade agreements. This decision may force them to look beyond the EU into emerging markets such as India.

Survey in India: Survey participants from India have pointed out that the Indian packaging industry is witnessing a double digit growth. It is characterised by a few large players and a large number of small and medium enterprises. Large Indian packaging companies such as Uflex Limited, Polyplex Corporation Limited and Essel Propack Limited have presence in countries such as the UK, Germany and Poland, among others. These companies have state-of-the art research and development facilities. The large players in the packaging industry have introduced new technologies such as modified atmosphere packaging in the segment of fresh food packaging. However, these technologies are yet to be adopted on a larger scale and across the food processing sector.

The survey participants have also pointed out that most of the modern machinery for testing and packaging are imported from countries such as the Netherlands, Germany and Italy. At present, import from the UK is very limited. In the case of raw materials used for packaging such as polystyrene, polyethylene terephthalate, aluminium foil, etc., the packaging companies both import some of the raw materials and source others locally. Raw materials are imported from countries such as Japan and Thailand, and the share of the UK is low. Overall, the survey confirms that the UK share in India's trade of packaging machinery and raw materials is low and there is scope for increasing the trade.

The survey highlights that packaging industry in India is largely small and in the non-corporate/unorganised/informal sector. The players in the non-corporate sector have certain advantages over the corporate players due to which they can offer tough competition. First, companies in the corporate/formal sector have to pay more taxes, which also acts as a disincentive for scale expansion. Second, SMEs in the informal sector rely mostly on cheap raw materials and traditional technology which enables them to have a cost advantage over the larger corporate players. The SMEs may not strictly abide by the FSSAI standards for food packaging. They may not also be aware of the importance of packaging as both protective and marketing tools. However, they do have clientele since the large part of the food processing industry is also in the non-corporate sector. Moreover, given that only a small segment of the Indian agricultural produce is processed, and there are only a few players for food processing in the corporate sector, the corporate packaging industry has smaller clientele compared to the size of the market. Further, modern technology entails costs and therefore, corporate players are not able to compete on costs with some of the players in the unorganised sector.

The traditional methods used in food packaging by SMEs require minimal training. The small players do not generally offer any specialised training for packaging and rely on learning by doing. However, in case of operating modern equipment for technologies such as modified atmosphere packaging and freeze-thaw dehydration technology, large companies provide in-house training. Thus, the large companies have to entail a cost of training. These companies have also reported that they would prefer tying up with organisations such as IIP to offer short-term courses for specialised packaging.

Survey participants from both the UK and India have pointed out that India is witnessing a shift towards modern retail and food habits are changing towards processed food from fresh produce. Consumer awareness regarding food quality and standards is also increasing. Thus, the role of food packaging technology is expected to increase and modern technologies are expected to become widespread in the future. Further, the fresh food packaging segment is still characterised by food wastage and spoilage. This is due to the use of conventional packaging methods that are inefficient vis-à-vis modern methods such as modified atmosphere packaging. Thus, the survey respondents feel that there is scope for the UK companies to enter the processed food packaging segment as well as fresh food packaging segment. The next section discusses the possible areas of cooperation within the food packaging sector between India and the UK.

3.5 Areas of Cooperation and Go-to-Market Strategy

The primary survey highlights that Indian packaging industry is growing fast and characterised by a few large players and a number of smaller players. Although modern packaging technologies have been introduced in food packaging, the industry is still largely characterised by traditional methods of packaging. The presence of the UK companies in packaging industry is limited; only a few companies such as Bell Packaging Private Limited have presence in India (see Figure 3.3) while companies such as PG Paper Company Limited source raw materials from India. The survey shows that a number of companies from the UK are interested in exploring the Indian markets and in bringing in new technologies. However, they are waiting for some of the UK and global retailers and food manufacturers to enter the Indian market.

Based on the findings from the survey, this section discusses the potential areas of cooperation between India and the UK in packaging technology and provides a go-to-market strategy for the UK companies.

3.5.1 Areas of Cooperation

One of the potential areas of investments is flexible packaging. This segment is the fastest growing segment in India and with a focus on cost effectiveness, innovations in flexible packaging will play a major role in industry's future growth. Companies from the UK that specialise in flexible packaging can collaborate with domestic companies to enter the Indian markets.

As modern forms of packaging technologies are gaining prominence in India, there are opportunities for the UK companies in areas such as freeze-thaw dehydration technology, deep freeze technology, vacuum packaging, tetra packaging and injection moulded plastic container packaging. Survey respondents feel that there is scope for collaboration in anti-counterfeiting technology in packaging and in sharing of knowledge in labelling technologies. There is also scope for collaboration on RFID technology in packaging.

The Indian government has renewed focus on recycling and clean technology under the National Action Plan on Climate Change. There is scope for collaboration between India and the UK companies to reduce the carbon footprint of the food packaging industry. The UK companies can bring in their expertise in recycling techniques and eco-friendly packaging. India will benefit from the UK companies' expertise in green packaging technology and in this area there is scope for business-to-business collaborations.

Another area of opportunity is the fresh food packaging segment. The survey has found that the Indian consumers have a higher preference for fresh produce over processed and packaged food products. They like to cook fresh vegetables, meat, etc. Further, the fresh food segment is characterised by high levels of wastage and spoilage due to traditional packaging methods. Modern packaging technologies, such as modified atmosphere packaging that help increase shelf life of perishable food products such as fruits, vegetables and meat products, can be introduced on a larger scale. Companies from the UK can invest in building capacity for these modern technologies.

The UK companies can source raw materials from India while packaging machinery manufacturers from the UK can export to India and invest in building modern packaging machinery units in India. Further, modern equipment require specialised handling. Hands-on-training and theoretical training to operate the machinery is another area where there is an opportunity for the UK companies. The UK companies can help in developing online modules and curricula for training in packaging technology. There is also scope for the UK companies to offer training to the Indian packaging companies in areas such as product handling and food safety.

3.5.2 Go to Market Strategy

In the recent years, the Indian government has come up with several polices and schemes that aim to promote manufacturing and can help facilitate the establishment of manufacturing facilities by the UK companies in India. The UK companies can look at the schemes and policies discussed in Section 3.5.1 and conduct a market feasibility study to enter the Indian market. They can seek support from business organisations such as the UKIBC that provides company specific market entry, research, and expansion services for the UK companies looking to enter Indian market.

Success of a foreign company in India depends on identifying the right state for establishing presence. There are 29 states in India and state-level policies play a key role in issues such as land acquisition, environmental and labour clearances, among others. States also have specific policies and schemes for encouraging manufacturing industry, which are generally listed under their industrial policy or sector specific policy. The UK companies need to carefully examine the state-level policies and regulations before entering the Indian market.

The next step is to identify the right business partner. It is suggested that the UK companies should enter the Indian markets and operate on a joint venture model of business, at least for the initial years until they gain complete market knowledge. At the entry stage it will reduce the risk if the packaging companies have some pre-existing clientele. The packaging companies can work with the UK retailers such as Tesco Plc and Indian retailers such as Future Group who are developing their own brands.

India has signed a number of trade agreements with countries, such as ASEAN member countries, Sri Lanka, Japan and Korea. India is also engaged in a number of trade negotiations which are likely to bring down the tariffs for packaging raw materials and machineries. The tariff reductions for raw material and packaging equipment under these trade agreements have to be carefully examined by the UK companies so that they can set up the most efficient production network.

The UK companies can also seek membership of IIP, which will enable them to understand the Indian market. Further, the UK companies can collaborate with the IIP to provide short-term training modules for specialised packaging. IIP can organise seminars, packaging exhibitions, etc., that can provide a platform for the UK companies to exhibit their technologies and seek collaborations with Indian companies. UKTI and UKIBC can explore the possibility of joint event and road shows with IIP.

Section

4

Skill Development in Food Supply Chain

One of India's major strengths vis-à-vis the developed countries such as Japan, Germany and the UK is its large young population. With almost 94 per cent of the population below the age of 64 years in 2015,[1] India has the largest youth population in the world. To reap the benefits of this demographic dividend, an educated and skilled workforce is required. Around 12.8 million people enter the workforce every year in India. However, the annual training capacity of the country is less than half of that (Infrastructure Development Finance Company, 2012). Further, it is estimated that in India, only 4.69 per cent of the total workforce has undergone any formal skill training (Ministry of Skill Development and Entrepreneurship [MSDE], 2015). Thus, skill development assumes a great importance in sustaining India's growth trajectory.

The Government of India has recognised the urgent need to harness India's demographic dividend through a skilled workforce. A major step towards this has been the creation of MSDE in the year 2014 to facilitate and align skill development initiatives throughout the country. The government is also keen on private sector investment and participation in training and skill development. India is seeking collaborations from foreign governments in its endeavour to uplift the skill levels.

One of the areas requiring skill development is the food supply chain. It has been discussed in the previous sections that India is one of the largest producers of most fruits and vegetables in the world but a substantial part of the produce get wasted in the supply chain due to several reasons including manhandling. Therefore, there is need for trained manpower across the different segments of the food supply chain. Further, in the past, food supply chain in India was fragmented and in the non-corporate/informal sector, which largely employed unskilled workers. However, with the development of modern storages, automated warehouses, packaging technology and cold-chains, the sector is moving towards corporatisation and there is a need for training of workforce to run sophisticated technology.

A number of studies have highlighted that there are shortages of refrigerated vehicles, modern pack-houses, automated warehouses, etc., (for example, see NCCD, 2015), which will in turn require trained personnel to run refrigerated vehicles, multi-temperature controlled warehouses, modern inventory tracking devices, forklift, among other tasks.

1. *https://www.cia.gov/library/publications/the-world-factbook/geos/in.html* (accessed on 4 March 2016).

In the area of packaging, food packaging is highly technical and needs trained workforce to maintain quality, reduce wastage and operate sophisticated machines for upcoming technologies in India such as green packaging technology, freeze-thaw dehydration technology, deep freeze technology, vacuum packaging, tetra packaging and injection moulded plastic container packaging.

Given this background, this section focuses on skill development in the food logistics sector in India. While a number of studies have focused on skill gaps in logistics sector or in the food processing sector (for example, see KPMG, 2007), there is hardly any study on skill gaps in food supply chain logistics sector. This section aims to fill that lacuna. The layout of the section is as stated below.

The first sub-section discusses the skill requirements in logistics focusing on three key areas within food supply chain logistics sector, namely storage and warehousing, cold-chain and packaging technology. Sub-section 4.2 examines the status of skills in food supply chain logistics in India. It identifies the existing skill gaps within food supply chain logistics sector and highlights the different private initiatives undertaken in the sector. Sub-section 4.3 focuses on the governance structure and regulations in the area of skill development in India. Sub-section 4.4 highlights the existing collaborations and initiatives in the area of skill development between India and the UK. The last sub-section presents the survey results and highlights the areas of collaboration and the go-to-market strategy for the UK businesses.

4.1 Skills Required in Food Supply Chain

International Standard Classification of Occupation classifies skills broadly into four levels, which are also applicable to skills required food supply chain logistics (see Figure 4.1).

As highlighted earlier, food supply chain logistics sector in India is modernising. This has resulted in the shift of demand from skill level 1 towards skill levels 2, 3 and 4, which require specialised training. As the demand for skilled workforce increases, the supply of skilled personnel has to scale up through training institutes and centres offering vocational training to meet the requirement. Further, the food logistics sector is moving from an in-house staff that manages inventory to complex 3PL and fourth party logistics (4PL) across domestic and international locations. Thus, there are now specialised companies for providing food logistics who require skilled workforce.

Figure 4.1

Skill Levels in Food Supply Chain

Skill Levels	Coverage & Requirement	Examples in the food supply chain logistics
Skill Level 1	Involves performance of simple and routine physical and manual tasks. Generally, completion of primary education is a pre-requisite and in some cases, a short period of on-the-job training may be required.	Porter, Freight Handler
Skill Level 2	Involves performance of tasks such as operating machinery and electronic equipment, driving vehicles and maintenance of mechanical equipment among others. Generally, first stage of secondary education is pre-requisite and some occupations require vocational education and on-the-job training.	Reefer Truck Driver
Skill Level 3	Involves performance of complex technical and practical tasks that require an extensive body of factual, technical and procedural knowledge in a specialised field. Generally, higher education of 1-3 years after completion of secondary education is a requirement for an occupation to fall under this category.	Warehouse Manager, Truck Mechanic
Skill Level 4	Involves performance of tasks that require complex problem-solving, decision making and creativity based on an extensive body of theoretical and factual knowledge in a specialised field. Generally, higher education of 3-6 years upon completion of secondary education that results in award of first degree is required.	Logistics/Sales Manager

Source: International Labour Organization (ILO), (2012).

A number of studies have highlighted that skilled workforce is needed in the supply chain to reduce inefficiencies and operate modernised equipment (for example, see PwC, 2012).

NSDC classifies logistics sector into three core segments: warehousing, transportation and value-added services (packaging, labelling and other auxiliary activities) (NSDC, 2009). Skill requirements vary across these segments. Within food supply chain logistics, this section focuses on the skills required in the storage and warehousing, cold-chain and packaging technology.

In the warehousing sector, specific skills are required at all levels ranging from operators such as forklift operators to managerial levels such as warehouse management. Training for such specialised workforce is provided both on-the-job and through established institutions. Traditional porters are now being replaced by crane operators for bulk handling. These operators require specialised skills such as knowledge of the forklift operations. Loading and warehouse supervisors require skills such as handling inventory management software, data entry as well as understanding of modern techniques of loading and unloading. Specialised knowledge is also required to operate RFID technology and bar coding, among others.

Cold-chain requires specialised skills such as engineers and technicians to handle cold storage equipments. Cold-chain sector also requires skilled personnel for handling multi-chamber, multi-temperature control storages and drivers for multi-temperature refereed vehicles. Further, cold-chains require operators capable of conducting quality checks and maintaining food safety and standards. With the technological improvements, existing skill sets also need to be upgraded. For example, to run a refrigerated truck, a truck driver not only has to have relevant driving experience but should also be competent in operating the global positioning system (GPS) and have the knowledge of temperature control systems.

In the area of packaging technology, conventional techniques of packaging such as corrugated box packaging require minimal skills whereas technological advancements in packaging such as introduction of nanotechnology enabled packaging require specialised knowledge to handle new equipment and raw materials. Further, upcoming technologies such as green packaging technology, freeze-thaw dehydration technology, deep freeze technology, vacuum packaging, tetra packaging, injection moulded plastic container packaging, modified atmosphere packaging etc., require specialised skills and knowledge. With the introduction of these modern technologies, specialised on-the-job training to handle these equipment is required.

At the managerial level, there is requirement for personnel with specialised degree or diploma in supply chain management. Many educational and vocational training institutes offer degree and diploma courses in supply chain management.

Thus, food supply chain logistics sector requires a wide range of skills. As India progresses towards 3PL and 4PL services in supply chain management, and the network of food supply chain logistics strengthens, demand for specialised skills is expected to increase in the future. The next section discusses the present state of skill development in India and skill gaps in the food logistics supply chain.

4.2 Status of Skill Development in India

This section covers the trends and patterns in the skill development sector in India. It provides data on the skill level of the country followed by an overview of the skill gap.

4.2.1 Trends in Skill Development in India

The proportion of economically active population (15-59 years) has increased from 57.7 per cent to 63.3 per cent of the total population during 1991 to 2013.[2] The labour force participation rate in 2013 was estimated to be 52.5 per cent.[3] According to a KPMG (2014) report, logistics sector in India employed around 16.74 million people in 2013 and the number is expected to increase to about 28.4 million by 2022.

Despite a large working force, the level of vocational training is low in India. According to the National Sample Survey (NSS) 66th Round, 73 per 1000 people in the age group 15-59 have received or were receiving formal or non-formal vocational training in the year 2009-10.[4] As can be seen in Figure 4.2, non-formal training is further segregated into different categories based on the source of training.

Figure 4.2

Per 1000 Distribution of Persons in the Age Group '15-59' with Vocational Training (2009-10)

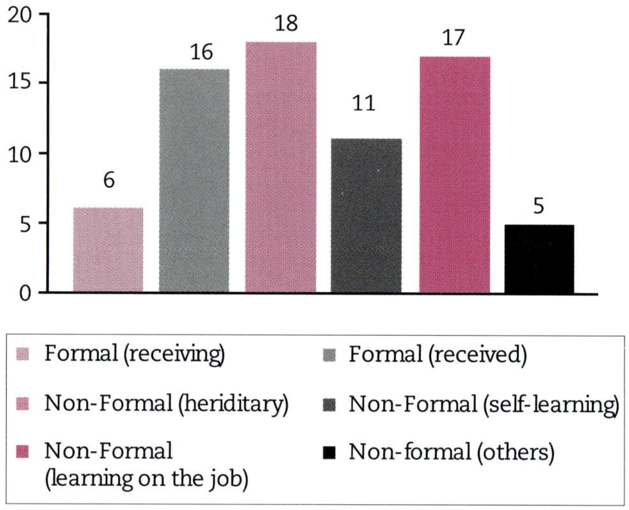

Source: Compiled from National Sample Survey Office (2013: 39, Statement 3.19).

Further, training varies across rural and urban population, males and females, and across different religious groups. For example, among the rural population who have received formal training, 113 per 1000 received the training for 'Driving and Motor Mechanic Work' whereas in the case of urban population, 307 out of 1000 people have received training for 'Computer Trades'. Industrial Training Institutes (ITIs) have been the foremost institutions in imparting vocational training throughout the country with 233 out of 1000 people being trained by ITIs or Industrial Training Centres (ITCs) (NSSO, 2013). Training infrastructure in terms of government ITIs as well as ITCs run by private sector has seen a significant increase from about 5,114 in 2007 to 9,447 in 2012. The seating capacity in these institutes has increased from 7.42 lakhs to 13.35 lakhs in the same period.[5]

Employment in the Indian logistics sector is also growing. Table 4.1 provides sector-wise employment projections in the logistics sector. Regions with the maximum employment in the transportation and

2. Ministry of Finance (2015).
3. Ministry of Labour and Employment (2014). Note that the estimation is done by Usual Principal Status approach. The other approach, Usual Principal and Subsidiary Status approach shows labour force participation rate to be 55.6 per cent.
4. *http://mospi.nic.in/Mospi_New/upload/nss_report_551.pdf* (accessed on 30 September 2015).
5. *http://mhrd.gov.in/sites/upload_files/mhrd/files/document-reports/XIIFYP_SocialSector.pdf* (accessed on 27 September 2015).

logistics sector as identified by the NSS 68th Round are Mumbai, Kolkata, Hyderabad, Delhi and Ahmedabad (KPMG, 2014).

Table 4.1

Employment in the Logistics Sector

Sector	Employment (in millions)		
	2013	2017*	2022*
Courier services	0.23	0.30	0.36
Packaging	0.22	0.26	0.30
Passenger railways	0.83	1.11	1.35
Passenger transport (roadways)	9.10	12.59	15.60
Rail freight	0.13	0.18	0.22
Road freight	5.79	7.99	9.88
Warehousing	0.43	0.57	0.69

Note: * refers to projections.

Source: KPMG (2014: 65).

4.2.2 Skill Gaps in Food Supply Chain Logistics

Studies on skills requirements in logistics highlight that there are skill gaps in the logistics sector and a number of factors are responsible for the low skill levels in this sector. These include fragmented nature of the business, high competition, poor working conditions and relatively less pay, among others (KPMG, 2014; NSDC, 2009).These studies also highlight that the current levels of expertise, vocational skills and management skills in the sector will not be able to meet the future demand of the logistics.

Skill gaps are present in the areas of warehousing, packaging technology and cold-chain. In the past, warehousing sector in India was characterised by traditional warehouses known as godowns. Over time, with the developments in logistics sector, automated warehousing is increasing. These warehouses provide both storage and value-added services. Growth in modern warehousing has created the need for specialised skills in operating modern machinery, providing value-added services such as sorting, labelling, grading and inventory management services. There is a lack of skilled workforce to run automated warehouses and provide client services (NSDC, 2009).

In the road transportation segment, drivers are not formally trained in handling heavy weight vehicles and refrigerated trucks. Moreover, Indian truck drivers usually have minimum education and they find it difficult to run complicated refrigerated vehicles with multiple temperature control and GPS technologies. There is need for formally trained drivers capable of driving refrigerated trucks, maintaining consistent temperatures and operating GPS and other technologies.

In the packaging sector, with the introduction of modern technology in food packaging such as modified atmospheric packaging, trained workforce to handle these equipment will be required.

4.2.3 Some Initiatives in Skill Development

Given the large population, which need employment and considering the skill gaps in various industries including food supply chain logistics, the Government of India has given priority to skill development. It is encouraging private sector to build capacity for skill development. Some of the notable initiatives are given in Box 4.1.

4.3 Governance Structure of Skill Development in India

In India, the government plays a key role in skill development and this is now a priority area for the government. As of 2015, over 70 skill development schemes across various sectors were being implemented by over 20 central ministries/departments.[6] The governance structure of skill development in India is cross-cutting and spans across various ministries, organisations and institutions at the centre and state government levels. The governance structure can be broadly viewed from three perspectives: promotion and facilitation of skill development, accreditation and curriculum designing, and skill training and educational institutes.

4.3.1 Promoting Skill Development through Institutions and Policies

Government initiatives for vocational training can be traced back to 1950 when the Directorate General of Employment & Training under the Ministry of Labour and Employment initiated Craftsmen Training Scheme by establishing about 50 ITIs for imparting skills in various vocational trades to meet the skilled manpower requirements. In 1956, National Council for Vocational Training (the then National Council of Training in Vocational Trades) was set up as an advisory body to the central government. The Council has been entrusted with the responsibilities of prescribing standards and curricula for craftsmen

6. *http://www.swaniti.com/wp-content/uploads/2015/06/Skill-development-Brief-Final-Version.pdf* (accessed on 29 September 2015).

Box 4.1

Private Initiatives for Skill Development

Confederation of Indian Industry (CII) Institute of Logistics: CII Institute of Logistics was established in 2004 as a Centre of Excellence in Logistics and Supply Chain. It offers workshops, training programmes and skill enhancement programmes in supply chain management and logistics. Some of its courses include diploma and certificate courses in supply chain management and logistics management. Further, CII Institute of Logistics also partners with industry to offer corporate training programs in areas such as warehouse management and supply chain performance analysis metrics, among others.

TeamLease University: It is the first skill university in India situated in Gujarat. It is an outcome of an MoU between TeamLease Services Private Limited and the Government of Gujarat to set up a private university for vocational education. The university offers degree programmes as well as runs an apprenticeship programme, National Employability through Apprenticeship Program. It is a PPP of TeamLease Skills University, CII, and NSDC under the National Employability Enhancement Mission of the MHRD. It focuses on "Learning by doing" and "Learning while earning" for the youth trainees along with providing them with access to practical skills.

Infrastructure Leasing & Financial Services (IL&FS) Skills Development Corporation: IL&FS Skills Development Corporation is a joint venture between IL&FS and NSDC and is one of the largest vocational training companies in India. It has a mandate to train 4 million people by 2022 through a network of 100 multi-skill institutes and 300 single skill schools . Skill development programmes are offered in 74 trades with duration ranging from 45 days to 6 months. IL&FS Skills Development Corporation works with a network of more than 1,500 employers to secure placement linkages before the start of the skill development programme. This ensures jobs for trainees and it also ensures that the supply of skilled manpower is in line with the industry demands.

Indian Institute of Materials Management (IIMM): IIMM focuses on logistics and related training. IIMM is a professionally recognised body of material management that offers skill development courses in supply chain management for 10+2 students under Skill Development Initiative Scheme of MSDE. The courses offered include logistics management, materials management and stores management, among others. The courses range from diploma in store management to Masters of Business Administration in Supply Chain Management.

Other Initiatives: NGOs have also been active in promoting skill development. One such example is Pratham Education Foundation. It is an educational NGO established in 1995 and is one of the biggest NGOs in the country. It offers vocational training to students from various rural areas, urban slums, and minority communities across India. The training period is usually 3 months in sectors such as hospitality, construction, and automotive, among others. Besides industry specific training, Pratham Education Foundation has also set up general skilling centres along with options in specific courses like retail, mobile repair and driving, among others. Some other niche segment training providers include Forklift Academy of India. It is the first forklift training school in India that offers hands-on training for all levels of forklift operator. The training period varies from one day for experienced operators and four to six days for fresh operators.

Source: Compiled from the websites of different organisations.

training, advising the government on the overall policy and programmes, conduct All India Trade Tests and awarding National Trade Certificates.[7] In the past, both Ministry of Human Resource Development (MHRD) and Ministry of Labour and Employment were responsible for skill development along with other central ministries and state governments. In 2014, a nodal ministry for skill development, MSDE was created to focus on skill development in India. The institutions for skill development, namely National Skill Development Agency (NSDA), NSDC and Directorate General of Training, which were under other ministries or functioning as autonomous bodies have now come under MSDE.

Although, various institutions were created for skill development, the sector received a focused attention in the Eleventh Five Year Plan (2007-2012). In 2009, the government announced a National Policy on Skill Development which laid down the framework for skills-related training. It identified roles of various stakeholders such as trade unions, government and industry to help promote skill development in India. The policy outlined the institutional structure at the national level for skill development. It led to the setting up of NSDC in 2009. NSDC is a not-for-profit company

7. *http://dget.nic.in/content/innerpage/national-council-on-vocational-training-ncvt.php* (accessed on 29 September 2015).

Box 4.2

National Skill Development Corporation (NSDC)

NSDC is a not-for-profit company set up by the Ministry of Finance in the year 2009. It is a PPP, which was set up to promote and fund private training providers as well as to set up private skill development centres. It has an equity base of INR 100 million, of which the Government of India holds 49 per cent, while the private sector has the balance 51 per cent. NSDC provides funding to build scalable, for-profit vocational training initiatives. Its mandate is also to enable support systems such as quality assurance, information systems and train the trainer academies either directly or through partnerships. NSDC has 37 Sector Skill Councils (SSCs) and 2 more are under formation.

SSCs are industry-led bodies that help bring the industry, labour and academia together for a specific sector. One such example is the Logistics Skill Council which is run by CII. Some of the areas under logistics identified for skill development by this council are material handling equipment, warehousing operations, trucking operations and packaging technologies, among others.

SSCs are responsible for development of National Occupation Standards and Qualification Packs for various job roles in a sector. Apart from the SSCs, NSDC has 203 training partners, which include for-profit and not-for-profit entities. These partners provide skill training throughout the country and are supported by NSDC.

Source: http://www.nsdcindia.org/ (accessed on 6 October, 2015).

of the government of India set up through a PPP route to help facilitate skill development initiatives and increase private sector involvement in this area (for details on NSDC, see Box 4.2).

The Twelfth Five Year Plan (2012-2017) of the erstwhile Planning Commission had set the target of creation of 50 million non-farm employment opportunities and provision of skill certification to at least equivalent number of people. In 2013, NSDA was set up as an autonomous body to coordinate and harmonise the skill development efforts of the government and the private sector to achieve the skilling targets of the Twelfth Five Year Plan. NSDA has been actively involved in collaborations with organisations such as the World Bank, the Asian Development Bank and the British Council to enhance the skill development in India. Other initiatives of NSDA include Prime Minister Skill Development Fellowship[8] and developing Labour Market Information System.[9]

The government has also introduced several schemes to build capacity for skill development in India. One such scheme is the Pradhan Mantri Kaushal Vikas Yojana. This scheme aims to offer 2.4 million Indian youth, industry relevant and skill-based training. Trainees are offered financial reward and a government certification upon completion of the training. As of 1 March 2016, the enrolments under this scheme stood at 1,527,527 while the number of trainings completed was 926,440.[10]

Apart from the central government initiatives, state governments have been actively promoting and facilitating skill development. State Skill Development Missions have been set up by almost every state and union territory. One such example is the Gujarat State Skill Mission that has been set up by the Government of Gujarat to bring together schemes of various departments, to avoid duplication or overlap and to strengthen quality of skill training. In addition, Gujarat Knowledge Society under the Government of Gujarat has a major programme of conducting skill trainings to enhance employability in the existing buildings of schools and colleges. The Society has a target of training 100,000 youth per year.[11] State specific policies on skill development have also been initiated. For instance, the Government of Karnataka formulated its state policy on skill development in 2008. This policy aims to ensure adequate availability of skilled manpower for micro enterprises, small scale, medium

8. Prime Minister Skill Development Fellowship is a scheme that provides work-cum-learning opportunity to young professionals interested in working in the skills sector at the state and district level. The fellows assist the State Skill Development Missions and the district administration in select districts and act as Skill development facilitators particularly in implementation of the flagship skill development schemes and generating greater participation of youth into the skill development/training programmes.
9. The Labour Market Information System is a labour market policy instrument that collects, evaluates and provides labour market information to both the labour supply side and the labour demand side. It helps assess the quantum of skill gaps in different sectors and provide policy suggestions to scale up or down infrastructure accordingly.
10. *http://www.pmkvyofficial.org/Index.aspx* (accessed on 1 March 2016).
11. *http://gujaratinformation.net/showpage.aspx?contentid=113* (accessed on 28 September 2015).

scale and large scale industrial clusters including SEZs and industrial parks.[12]

The most recent initiative of the central government is the National Policy for Skill Development and Entrepreneurship 2015, which supersedes the National Policy on Skill Development of 2009. The policy aims to provide an umbrella framework to all skilling activities being carried out in the country, to align them to common standards and link skilling with demand centres. The policy envisages to promote national skills universities and institutes in partnership with states as centres of excellence for skill development and training of trainers, either as de-novo institutions or as a part of existing university landscape. Under the policy, companies are encouraged to spend at least 25 per cent of their Corporate Social Responsibility (CSR) funds[13] on skill development initiatives directly or through the national Skill Development Fund.[14] It also recommends industry to earmark 2 per cent of its payroll bill for skill development initiatives in their respective sectors. Further, government schemes across sectors are encouraged to apportion a certain percentage of the scheme budget towards skilling of human resources.

4.3.2 Accreditation and Curriculum Designing

Since the setting up of NSDC, there has been a focus on accreditation and curriculum designing in close association with industry and sector experts. With multiple stakeholders and various certifications in skill development in India, the government has tried to align the different certifications into a single framework, National Skills Qualification Framework (NSQF). This framework organises qualifications according to a series of levels of skills, knowledge and aptitude. It helps facilitate mobility from vocational to general education and vice-versa. NSQF is composed of ten levels representing different levels of complexity and knowledge required to demonstrate competence commensurate for that level. Apart from NSQF, National Occupational Standards define the measurable performance outcomes required in various vocations. These standards form the benchmarks for various education and training programmes and recruitment of human resource management practices.

The Directorate General of Training under MSDE is responsible for the development and coordination at national level for the programmes relating to vocational training including women's vocational training and employment services. Employment service is operated through a countrywide network of employment exchanges.

Under the Directorate General of Training, National Council for Vocational Training prescribes standards and curricula for craftsmen training, advises the Government of India on the issues relating to policy and programmes, conducts All India Trade Tests and awards National Trade Certificates. It prescribes standards in respect of syllabi, equipment, and scale of space, duration of courses and methods of training. It recognises training institutions run by government or by private agencies for purposes of the grant of National Trade Certificates and lays down conditions for such recognition. It also prescribes the standards and conditions of eligibility for the award of National Trade Certificates.

In addition, vocational training institutes such as ITIs require accreditation from National Accreditation Board for Education and Training. The latter is a constituent Board of Quality Council of India and is responsible for handling the scheme of accreditation of government and private ITIs.

4.3.3 Skill Training and Educational Institutes

There are several government institutes for vocational training such as ITIs and Advanced Training Institutes among others (see Box 4.3). In addition to these institutes, polytechnics, National Institute of Open Schooling, and community colleges provide vocational training in India. Central Board of Secondary Education also offers 34 vocational courses consisting of 107 subjects in about 500 of its government and government aided schools across the country.[15]

Thus, the government plays a key role in designing the framework and accreditation of vocational training and skill education in India. It also promotes and facilitates skill development initiatives by private players alongside its own initiatives. Further, the government also encourages international investments and collaboration in the area of skill development.

12. *http://planningcommission.gov.in/reports/genrep/skilldev/10_noti/Karnataka%20SkillPolicy.pdf* (accessed on 28 September 2015).
13. An example of the CSR initiative is that of Chola Madalam Investment and Finance Company Limited. Through NSDC, Chola Madalam Investment and Finance Company Limited has contributed INR5 million towards skill development in the automotive and banking sectors.
14. National Skill Development Fund was set up in 2009 for raising funds both from government and non-government sector for skill development in the country.
15. *http://mhrd.gov.in/nveqf* (accessed on 30 September 2015).

Box 4.3

Institutes for Vocational Training

Industrial Training Institutes (ITIs): These are the oldest institutes imparting vocational training in India. As mentioned earlier, the first 50 ITIs were set up in 1950 under the Craftsmen Training Scheme. Initially began as government institutes, presently ITIs are both government-owned and privately-owned. At present there are a total of 11,964 (2284 government and 9680 private) ITIs in India. Training is imparted in 126 trades forduration 1-2 years.

Advanced Training Institutes and Model Industrial Training Centres (MITIs): These institutes aim to train instructors the technique of transferring hands-on skill in order to train semi-skilled/skilled manpower for industry. At present, there are 6 Advanced Training Institutes across India. MITIs conduct restructured patterns of Craftsmen Training Programme on modular basis. At present, there are 4 MITIs across India.

NSDC Affiliated Training Providers: There are 203 training providers affiliated to NSDC which include for-profit and not-for-profit entities. Two types of courses are affiliated under NSDC:

- Courses conducted by NSDC approved training partners which should be certified by SSCs as well as courses that may not be certified by SSCs as no SSC exists in that area.
- Courses certified by SSCs which are not provided by NSDC funded training partners.

Source: *http://www.dget.nic.in/content/innerpage/overview-cts.php* (accessed on 29 September 2015); *http://www.nsdcindia.org/our-affiliates-0* (accessed on 30 September 2015).

Box 4.4

Select International Collaborations and Areas of Cooperation for Skill Development

India has several initiatives with Germany in skill development. The Ministry of Labour and Employment, the Government of India and the Federal Ministry of Education and Research of the Federal Republic of Germany signed an MoU in 2011 in the area of vocational education and training. It led to the formation of a Joint Working Group to foster partnerships and review progress in the field of vocational education and training. The Joint Working Group focuses on designing competency based curriculum with engagements from German experts.

Another example of Indo-German collaboration in the field of skill development is the Karnataka German Multi Skill Development Centre. It is a society promoted by the Government of India and the Government of Karnataka with technical support of German International Services. It has set up Karnataka German Technical Training Institute having centres at Bangalore, Belgaum, Hubli, Mangalore and Gulbarga. All programmes follow German vocational education and training standards. It offers courses in areas such as welding and information technology, among others.

India has collaborated with Singapore in the area of vocational education and skill development. The areas of cooperation include capability development in vocational education and skill development, advisory services by Institute of Technical Education (Singapore) to enhance planning, management and delivery of vocational education and skill development in India and other areas such as linking ITIs (India) and Institute of Technical Education (Singapore).

The MoU between US-India Business Council and the NSDC was signed in November 2014 to facilitate US companies to set up and/or support skill development centres in India. As part of the collaboration US-India Higher Education Cooperation administered a grant to Montgomery College to help build capacity in the vocational and technical education sector in India. The project intends to develop community college models appropriate for India. It focuses specifically on faculty development and training, aligning training programmes with local and emerging industry, and organising an online symposium on topics related to the growth and development of community colleges in India.

Source: Information provided by Indian government officials and industry associations.

Box 4.5

India-UK Collaboration in Skill Development

UK-India Education and Research Initiative (UKIERI): UKIERI is a multi-stakeholder programme established in 2006 where both the countries engage in mutually beneficial opportunities in the education and research and development fields. The aim is to learn from UK's valuable experience in developing skills and to intensify bilateral engagements in skill development. UKIERI is about to commence its third phase (2016-21). The previous two phases (2006-11, 2011-16) have focussed on areas including skill development and innovation partnerships, among others. In the area of skill development, its objective is to enable the development of a strong Indian sector skills infrastructure focusing on employer engagement approaches, developing curriculum and qualifications, certification and assessment, etc.

Joint Working Group-India UK Partnership on Skills:The Joint Working Group on Education and Skills was established in 2005 as a point for the collaboration and partnership between the two countries on skills and education with the objective that the organisations in India and the UK can work together to address India's skilled manpower challenge while maximising mutual business growth opportunities in highly innovative and output driven ways.

Key focus areas of the Joint Working Group are:

- Indian companies' participation in the UK skills and training market.
- Vocational education in schools.
- Capacity building and quality management.
- Leadership development programmes.
- Cross-sectoral collaborations.

UK India Skills Forum:It is anindustry led implementation group that acts as a 'one stop shop' for organisations in India and the UK interested in doing business together. The forum is a first contact point for industry partners on both sides which support the Indian members to acquire best of knowledge and reach. It is guided by two co-chairs, each representing the managing partners, FICCI and UKIBC in the UK.

It acts as platform for exchange of ideas, sharing of best practices, structuring strategic dialogue, recognising the contributions and facilitating sustainable business partnerships. It has supported various roundtables, delegation and business visits and summits educating companies from both the sides about the business opportunities, challenges and possible solutions. It focuses on knowledge transfer to promote benchmarking around curriculum framework and trainer development through training of trainers and accreditation of trainers.

Source: http://www.ukieri.org/ (accessed on 8 March 2016); http://www.ukisf.com/INDIA-UK-Partnership.pdf (accessed on 8 March 2016); *http://ukisf.com/* (accessed on 8 March 2016).

The next section discusses the present international collaborations in the area of skill development.

4.4 International Collaborations and Areas of Cooperation in Skill Development

Skill development has also received attention through international collaborations. India has been engaged with countries such as Australia, France, Germany, the UK and the US in vocational training, training of trainers, setting up of centres of excellence. Some of these initiatives are given in Box 4.4.

The Indian and the UK government have several collaborations in the area of skill development. The Ministry of Labour and Employment (India) and the Department for Business, Innovations and Skill (UK) have signed an MoU for cooperation in the area of skill development and employment services in 2013.[16] An MoU between NSDC and UK Commission on Employment and Skills was signed in 2011 for collaboration to support SSCs and other skill initiatives in India. Further, an MoU between NSDC and Association of Colleges, UK, was signed in 2014 for building training capacity and international benchmarking in certifications. Some of the other initiatives between India and the UK are given in Box 4.5.

India and the UK also have some private sector collaborations in skill development. A notable example

16. The MoU is available at *http://dget.nic.in/upload/uploadfiles/files/UKIERIMoU.pdf* (accessed on 29 March 2016).

is the collaboration between ThinkLink Supply Chain Services Private Limited and RTITB Limited (formerly Road Transport Industry Training Board). ThinkLink Supply Chain Services Private Limited is skill development company in the area of supply chain management and logistics. It operates in segments such as cold-chain, food and beverages, and consumer packaged goods, among others. RTITB Limited is a UK-based company that provides certification and training in forklift and reach truck operations. Under the Praguna initiative, ThinkLink has collaborated with RTITB to offer forklift training in India that has RTITB accreditation which allows the trainees to work in many countries since RTITB certification is recognised globally.

Another example of India-UK collaboration is the joint skill development centre of Manipal City & Guilds Private Limited. It was founded in 2009 by City & Guilds (UK) and Manipal Education Services (India). It offers skills training as well as certification for vocational training. It has a network of over 100 centres across 25 states. The training courses are offered in a wide range of sectors including supply chain management, retail and construction, among others. Manipal City & Guilds Private Limited has partnered with academic institutions, state governments, private players, government and NGOs to create a robust network of skill development. This network provides end-to-end solutions of bringing the industry curriculum, offering training, assessment, certification and placements to the students.

These examples show that India and the UK have been collaborating in the field of skill development. The next section discusses the scope of collaboration between India and the UK in food supply chain logistics.

4.5 Primary Survey

To examine the scope of India-UK collaboration in the area of skill development in food supply chain logistics, a primary survey of 20 stakeholders from the industry, industry bodies, skill development organisations and policymakers in India and the UK has been conducted.

In the primary survey, the respondents are asked to describe the evolving nature of food supply chain logistics in India, their assessment of the skill gaps and potential areas of collaboration between India and the UK. The UK respondents are asked to highlight their areas of specialisation, their potential collaborators in India and feasible forms of collaborations in the area of skill development in food supply chain logistics. All the respondents feel that there is a huge demand for skilled workforce in food supply chain logistics of India. The key drivers of this demand will be economic growth, liberalisation and reform initiatives of the government (such as liberalising FDI in multi-brand retail and implementation of the single goods and services tax), changes in consumer food habits and infrastructure development.

4.5.1 The Skill Gaps

The survey has found that there are skill gaps in all segments of food supply chain logistics. Within the food supply chain logistics, skill gaps are prominent in certain areas across different levels. For example, at the operational level, there is a shortage of trained forklift operators, whereas at the managerial level, there is a shortage of trained warehouse managers capable of handling automated warehouses. The survey participants have pointed out that the food logistics sector is growing at a double digit rate and with the entry of organised players and domestic and global manufacturers and retailers, the industry is moving towards integrated 3PL and 4PL systems. There is a need for both in-house training and specialised training institutes to meet the future requirements of skilled workforce.

The survey finds that there is a shortage of training institutes for persons at the shop floor in warehouses, cold-chain, etc., especially for those who handle the products. Unless these people are trained, there will be wastage in food supply chain due to mishandling. Skill training is required to handle multi-chamber storages and run multi-temperature control vehicles. Skilled workforce is also needed to maintain food safety standards.

India is moving towards increased usage of automatic warehouses, which are now largely catering to retailers, distributors and large manufacturers. There is a need for training in automation, RFID technology, bar coding, perishable product handling and inventory management. Training in usage of warehouse equipment such as forklift, stackers and pallets is a potential area for investment. The survey finds that it is extremely difficult to get skilled or semi-skilled workforce for loading and unloading and in this area there is a skill gap.

In the case of packaging technology, there is a need for skilled workforce in areas such as green packaging, freeze-thaw dehydration technology, deep freeze technology, vacuum packaging, tetra packaging, injection moulded plastic container packaging, etc. There is a demand for skilled workforce in flexible packaging. With the introduction of modern techniques in food packaging such as modified atmosphere packaging, specialised on-the-job training to handle these equipment would be required. The IIP has started dedicated programmes in packaging technology. However, the survey shows that these are not enough to meet the requirement of skilled labour in handling sophisticated packaging equipment and machineries. There is also a need for training in labelling and food safety regulations across all segments of the food supply chain.

4.5.2 Areas of Collaborations

The survey shows that there is scope for collaboration in the areas of warehousing, cold-chain and packaging technology across different levels ranging from government-to-government collaborations to collaborations between two private companies or collaborations between academic institutions and private companies or among academic institutions of the two countries. The forms of collaboration can also vary ranging from a green field investment to set up joint skill development centre in food supply chain logistics to technical and academic support for existing skill development initiatives in India. Some of the potential collaborations found out during the survey are discussed below:

- Joint skill development centre: Survey respondents have pointed out that one of the most feasible forms of collaborations is through setting up of a joint skill development centre on a PPP model with an initial seed funding from the UK and Indian governments. A joint UK-India skill development centre in supply chain would enable to bridge the skill gaps in the specific segments of food supply chain logistics such as automated warehousing, cold-chain and packaging technology. It would bring together the technical expertise of the UK institutions and the infrastructure(such as concessional land) can be provided by the Indian state governments. Institutions from the UK can contribute in areas such as curriculum designing, training of the trainers and online distant training modules, among others. Training can be offered in the areas of skill gap as has been listed above.

  Specifically, in the warehousing segment, with the increasing levels of automations, there is a skill shortage to handle and operate modern equipment. The joint skill development centre can provide crafted training courses for areas such as forklift operations and online training modules for warehouse management systems, among others. In the area of cold-chain, the joint skill development centre can provide modules in the area of reefer truck driving. There is also scope for providing training to people who can track and monitor refrigerated vehicles. Further, skill training is required to handle multi-chamber and multi-temperature control vehicles. In the case of packaging technology, there is scope for offering training in areas listed above.

- Memorandums of Understanding (MoUs): Although India and the UK have signed several MoUs in the area of skill development since 2011; the two countries should sign an MoU on skill development in the area of food supply chain logistics. This MoU can focus on encouraging private collaborations and investments in areas such as automated warehousing, cold-chain, food safety and standards, and packaging technology. The MoU will show government interest and private sector will then respond to such MoUs.

- Technical support: Skill development institutes from the UK can offer comprehensive curricula and accreditation for industry specific job roles, which are recognised globally. Offering such recognition to training can help build a globally competent workforce in food logistics. Further, in areas such as operating warehouse management systems and handling of perishables among others, the UK companies and training institutes can offer online training modules with illustrated graphics for effective learning. The UK training institutes can also offer distant learning certificate courses. In the area of packaging technology, there is scope for collaboration between packaging training institutes in the UK such as Campden BRI and Indian institutes such as IIP. In the area of warehousing, specialised courses can be crafted in collaboration with Indian warehousing companies and industry associations. Collaboration can be made with the UKWA and Institute of Supply Chain Management, UK, for courses in automated warehouse management and other operator level courses.

- Training of trainers: One area of collaboration is providing training for the trainers. The private and government ITIs had a requirement of 60,000 instructors in the year

2011 with an expected demand of additional 5000 instructors per year.[17] Given the growing demand for qualified instructors, the UK companies can collaborate with ITIs and other skill development centres to provide training of trainers. Some of the potential collaborators from the UK are BRC Training Academy and Campden BRI. BRC certifies trainers who can deliver BRC training worldwide. It has certified companies such as NSF Safety and Certifications India Private Limited and SGS India Private Limited to make them approved trainers of BRC in India. BRC has 560 certificated sites in India, out of which 397 are certificated against the food standard, 141 against the packaging standards, 18 against consumer products and 4 against the storage and distribution standards. Thus, there is scope for BRC to contribute to training in India.

- Mutual recognition agreements, twinning programmes and certifications: Mutual recognition of degrees/diplomas obtained by trainees would help facilitate easier mobility across two countries. It can help UK obtain a young skilled workforce from India in the food logistics sector given its ageing workforce. Survey respondents have pointed out that certifications from UK institutes and recognition from universities in the UK can help in making Indian food supply chain logistics workforce globally competent and can ease cross-country mobility-related barriers, especially those related to recognition of training. The UK institutions in food logistics skill development can also offer twinning programmes to a pool of Indian trainees in the areas of automated warehousing, reefer truck driving and packaging technology, among others. Under the twinning programme, selected trainees can work in the UK for a short duration (3-6 months). These twinning programmes would help Indian workforce get exposure to international work culture and hands on experiences in operating modern machineries in food supply chain logistics. Indian skill development organisations can collaborate with universities such as the University of Hull and Brunel University, London to send supply chain professionals for short duration courses.

4.5.3 Go-to-Market Strategy for the UK Institution and Businesses

In skill development, the market entry for the UK companies has to be driven by the UK government. This is because skill, diploma, certification, etc., in India is largely under government initiatives. First, the Indian and UK governments can sign an MoU and in this regard UKTI can take a lead role in getting the MoU signed. Simultaneously, there is a need to have more interaction among businesses and training institutes of the two countries. These can be facilitated through exchange programmes, seminars and conferences. UKIBC can also help to do a feasibility study.

The UK businesses and training institutions not only need to identify the skill gaps, they also need to customise the curriculum and training modules to the need/demand of the Indian industry. Sometimes training may have to be provided in local language.

The best way to set up the training institute is through a PPP model where the Indian government provides concessional land or the Indian and the UK governments provide some seed funding. The initial investment can be large and the gestation period can be 5-6 years. Government support will help to reduce the risk.

India is a price sensitive country and ability to pay for training is much lower than in the UK. Therefore, the course fees have to be designed accordingly. The UK companies and institutes should target specialised training, training of trainers and training of persons already in the job. These people will have the ability to pay. They can enter into partnership with Indian companies for training of their employees. The UK companies may also explore the possibilities of offering training through the CSR funding of Indian companies.

Overall, this section shows that India and the UK have scope for collaboration in the area of skill development in food supply chain logistics. In India, skill development is a priority area and the government is actively seeking international investments. The UK companies and institutions are also keen to invest in this sector. However, there are some barriers, which are discussed in Section 6. These barriers need to be addressed to attract investments and collaborations from the UK. The Indian and the UK governments have to work together to address these barriers.

17 *http://www.dget.nic.in/content/institute/institutes-for-training-of-trainers-itots.php* (accessed on 9 October 2015).

Section 5

Research and Development in Food Logistics

The contribution of research & development (R&D) to economic progress is well-recognised. R&D is an essential input for technology and innovation. Countries across the world are undertaking R&D expenditure to have a sustainable growth and high income. Due to this, over the years, there has been an increase in the global R&D spending.

R&D can be in both product design and processes. With increasing globalisation and changes in demand, not only new products are being manufactured but substantial innovations are happening in the entire supply chain including manufacturing, transportation, warehousing, storage, packaging, just-in-time deliveries and marketing, among others. In food supply chain, R&D is required to maintain the quality of the products, reduce cost, maintain production schedule, ensure food safety and standards, and for inventory management and faster delivery. R&D helps a company to move ahead of its competitors through the use of right raw materials, technologies and processes. Companies from developed countries need R&D in food supply chain to enter developing country markets as the taste patterns, infrastructure, climate conditions and storages facilities may be different. R&D in developing countries is also required for improving logistics efficiencies, increasing the shelf life of products and reducing wastages especially in the supply chain. R&D in food supply chain is a cross-cutting issue and it plays an important role in improving the efficiency of storages and warehouses, cold-chains and food packaging. Innovation in each of these areas will help develop an efficient food supply chain.

This section has three sub-sections. The first sub-section presents the overview of the R&D sector in India including the patterns of spending, governance structure and applicable regulations. Sub-section 5.2 presents the scope for R&D collaborations and international partnerships. Finally, sub-section 5.3, highlights the primary survey findings.

5.1 Overview of the R&D Sector in India

This section highlights the pattern of spending in India and globally, the governance structure of the Indian R&D sector and the application regulations.

5.1.1 Pattern of Spending

In 2014, the global R&D expenditure was around 1.8 per cent of the world GDP.[1] Compared to this, the R&D spending is India is quite low. As per the Global Innovation Index for the year 2015, India was ranked 42nd with a gross expenditure on R&D (GERD) of only 0.81 per cent of the GDP while the UK was ranked 21st with a GERD of 1.73 per cent of the GDP in 2013. Israel and the Republic of Korea had the highest GERD, which was valued at 4.2 per cent of the GDP (see Figure 5.1). Further to this, India was ranked 81st among 141 countries while the UK was ranked second on the Global Innovation Index.[2]

The National Science and Technology Information Management Systems, Ministry of Science and Technology, the Government of India releases the official estimates of R&D spending in India. However, in India, the data collection mechanism is not very robust and often there is a lag in the release of information. The latest available data are for the FY[3] 2011-12, which show that the total R&D spending in India was around INR 726 billion in that year. Of this, around 30 per cent was funded by the private sector and the remaining by the public sector including the central government, state government and higher education institutions.[4]

International comparisons reveal that India has one of the lowest private sector contributions to R&D expenditure and R&D in India is largely funded by the government.[5] Compared to this, in most developed countries including the UK, a majority of the R&D is funded by the private sector (see Figure 5.2). As a result, the sectoral composition of the R&D in India reflects national priorities more than the business needs. In this context, India can learn from the UK on how to enhance the participation of private sector and higher institutions in R&D.

Regarding the sector-wise R&D spending, in 2009-2010, a majority of the public sector R&D expenditure in India was incurred on the defence sector (34%), followed by industrial machinery (29%), fuels (21%) and metallurgical industries (7%). Compared to this, a majority of the industrial R&D expenditure was incurred on drugs and pharmaceutical research (27.7%) followed by transportation, which includes commercial vehicles for movement of goods including

1. As per an advance estimate by Battelle (2013).

2. See Cornell University, INSEAD and World Intellectual Property Organization (WIPO) (2015).
3. In India, the FY spans from April to March, each year.
4. For details see *http://www.nstmis-dst.org/PDF/table1.pdf* (accessed on 19 September 2015).
5. Please note that there are minor discrepancies in the international data and the data available from domestic source. This is perhaps because the national data available is an estimate released by the Department of Science and Technology while the international data is the actual.

Figure 5.1

GERD as a Percentage of GDP in 2013 for Selected Countries

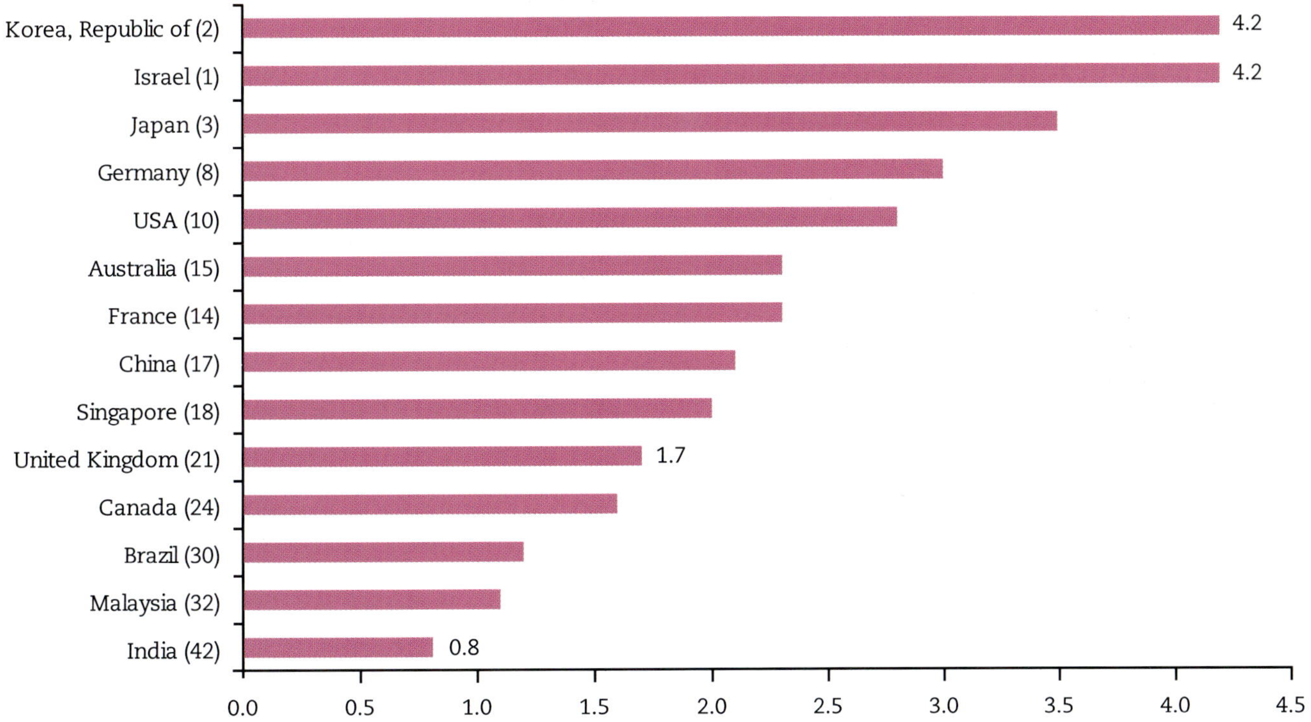

Note: The numbers in the parenthesis are the respective ranks of the countries in terms of the GERD among 141 countries.

Source: Compiled from Cornell University, INSEAD and WIPO (2015): 326, Table 2.3.2.

Figure 5.2

Distribution of the GERD by the Funding Agency in 2012 (in percentage)

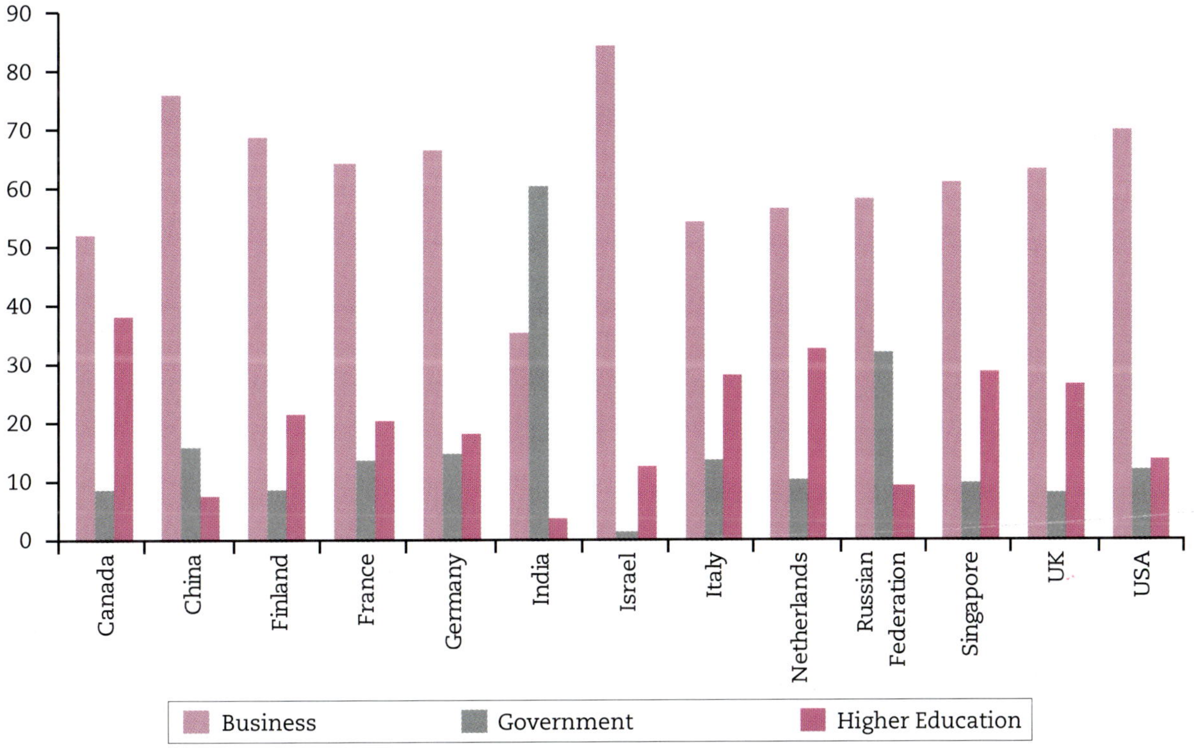

Source: Compiled from the United Nations Educational, Scientific and Cultural Organization (UNESCO) database on R&D available at: *http://www.uis.unesco.org/ScienceTechnology/Pages/research-and-development-statistics.aspx* (accessed on 19 September 2015).

food products (14%), information technology (13.6%) and defence industries (6.1%).[6] From this data, it is difficult to estimate the R&D spending specifically on the food logistics sector. Moreover, R&D in refrigerated transport or cold storage can benefit multiple sectors including food and pharmaceutical. Thus, benefits of R&D are often across sectors.

Till date, the R&D expenditure in India is mostly driven by the public sector. Within the public sector, the Department of Science and Technology and the Department of Biotechnology are the two key players contributing to nearly 50 per cent of the extramural R&D expenditure in India.[7] In this context, it is worth mentioning that although there is significant R&D in government institutions, there is a lack of commercialisation of R&D. It is important to understand the governance structure of the R&D sector in the country to have a better understanding of the role and responsibilities of the government in supporting R&D in India.

5.1.2 Governance Structure

R&D is a cross-cutting phenomenon and almost all ministries at the central government have a mandate and budget for technology adoption and development of more efficient methods of production and delivery in their respective fields. The R&D ecosystem in India consists of interconnected stakeholders, and includes central government ministries/agencies/departments, state government ministries/agencies/departments, autonomous bodies, universities, research institutions and private players.

At the centre, there are various ministries involved in R&D which include the Ministry of Science and Technology, MoFPI, the Ministry of Communications and IT, the Ministry of Defence (MoD), the Ministry of Agriculture and MoCI, among others. These ministries are involved in carrying out R&D work in their respective sectors. For example, under MoD, there is Defence Research and Development Organisation (DRDO), which does R&D related to defence technologies.

The Ministry of Science and Technology is the nodal ministry for formulation and administration of the rules and regulations relating to science and technology in India. The Ministry has three departments (see Figure 5.3). The three departments, namely the Department of Biotechnology (DBT), the Department of Science and Technology (DST) and the Department of Scientific and Industrial Research (DSIR), look after different aspects of the research and development, through their various councils, subordinate and attached offices.

Figure 5.3

Governance Structure of the Science and Technology Sector in India

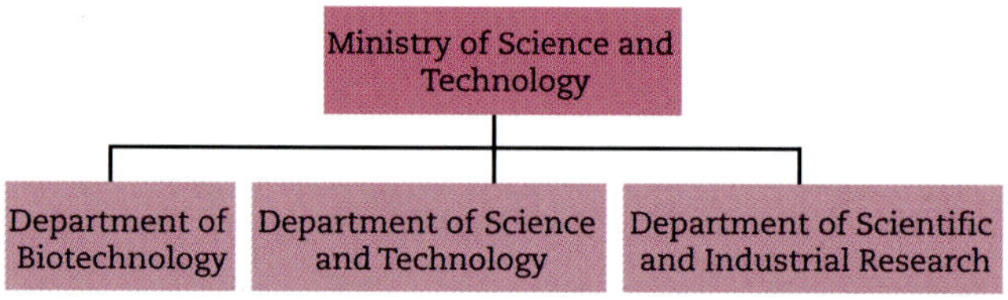

While the DBT largely focuses on biosciences-related research, it is the DST and the DSIR that focuses on other sectors that include research on supply chain and logistics-related areas. A brief overview of the three departments is given in Box 5.1.

Some of the government institutes and councils are undertaking or funding research on food logistics and supply chain. These departments are also entrusted with the task of formulating policies and promoting science and technology and research in their respective fields. In addition, there are a number of government funded testing laboratories that provide infrastructure and testing facilities across a wide array of sectors.

From time to time, the government announces science and technology policy. India has declared 2010-2020 as the decade of innovation. The Science, Technology and Innovation Policy 2013, aims to position India among the top five global scientific powers by 2020. It focuses on establishing world-class infrastructure for R&D, linking science, research and innovation system with inclusive growth, creating an environment to enhance private sector participation in R&D, encouraging PPP, among others. Science, Research and Innovation System for High Technology-led path for India (SRISHTI) is the main policy goal of the Science, Technology and Innovation Policy 2013. The policy also refers to gender equality and more participation of women in R&D. It refers to provision of incentives for commercialisation of innovation with focus on green manufacturing. The policy clearly reflects the growing focus of the Indian government to create an enabling environment to encourage private investments in the field of science and technology.

During the Eleventh Five Year Plan (2002-2007), the Science and Engineering Research Board, an

6. For details see Department of Science and Technology (2012). *http://www.nstmis-dst.org/PDF/Table12.pdf (accessed on 19 September 2015).*
7. Department of Science and Technology (2012).

Box 5.1

Brief Overview of DBT, DST and DSIR

Department of Biotechnology (DBT): DBT was set up to promote large scale use of biotechnology in the country and to support R&D and manufacturing in biology. The department has worked significantly in the application of biotechnology in the fields of agriculture, healthcare, animal sciences and environment. The mandate for DBT includes identification and setting up centres of excellence for R&D, integrating programme for human resource development, serving as nodal point for the collection and dissemination of information relating to biotechnology, and promoting large scale use of biotechnology, among others. Under DBT, there are multiple autonomous institutions that carry out respective advanced research work in various fields of biotechnology.

Department of Science and Technology (DST): DST was established with the objective of promoting new areas of Science & Technology and to play the role of a nodal department for organising, coordinating and promoting Science & Technology activities in the country. Major responsibilities include formulation of policies related to Science & Technology, promotion of new areas of Science and Technology with special emphasis on emerging areas, coordination and integration of areas of Science & Technology having cross-sectoral linkages in which a number of institutions and departments have interest and capabilities, support and provide grants-in-aid to scientific research institutions, scientific associations and bodies among others. There are multiple councils and sub-divisions under the department (for instance, the Science and Engineering Research Council).

Department of Scientific and Industrial Research (DSIR): The primary endeavour of DSIR is to promote R&D by the industries, support a larger cross-section of small and medium industrial units to develop state-of-the art globally competitive technologies of high commercial potential, catalyse faster commercialisation of R&D, enhance the share of technology intensive exports in overall exports, strengthen industrial consultancy and technology management capabilities and establish user friendly information network to facilitate scientific and industrial research in the country. It also provides a link between scientific laboratories and industrial establishments for transfer of technologies through National Research Development Corporation and facilitates investment in R&D through Central Electronics Limited. Just like DST, there are multiple councils under DSIR. For example, there is Council for Scientific and Industrial Research, National Aerospace Laboratories and National Automotive Testing and R&D Infrastructure Projects, among others.

Source: The websites of the different departments.

autonomous body under the Department of Science and Technology,was set up by an Act of the Parliament to promote research in science and technology and support researchers in this area. Besides financially supporting R&D projects of individual researchers and institutions, the Board has launched several new initiatives to improve access to state-of-the-art facilities.

Thus, promoting R&D has been one of the core objectives of the government. The new government has launched the 'Start-up India' campaign to attract investments and initiatives in R&D and innovation. However, there is still low commercialisation of R&D in the country due to the lack of a proper ecosystem for protection and promotion of R&D in India. Given this, it is important to understand the prevalent regulations in the sector.

5.1.3 R&D Regulations in India

A majority of the laws and regulations affecting the R&D sector are formulated and implemented by MoCI. Intellectual property rights (IPR) in India falls under the purview of Controller General of Patents, Designs & Trade Marks in the Department of Industrial Policy and Promotion (DIPP), MoCI. The organisational structure is given in Figure 5.4.

India's patent law is adopted from the British system. After independence, the focus of the Indian government was to increase patents by domestic companies as compared to foreign companies or proprietors. In the light of achieving this objective, the Patent Act 1970 was enacted. After India's accession to the World Trade Organization (WTO) in 1995, amendment to the India's Patent Act was enacted in 2005. This Act is compliant with the WTO's Trade-Related Aspects of Intellectual Property Rights Agreement. However, there is difference between India's patent regulation and regulation in other countries such as the US. In India, software is under copyright and is not patented, unlike many other countries.

Table 5.1 gives the trends in IPR granted over the past few years. The table reflects that there has been a notable decline in the number of patents granted in India while there has been an increase in designs, trade mark and geographical indications registered.

Figure 5.4

Organisational Details of Intellectual Property Office

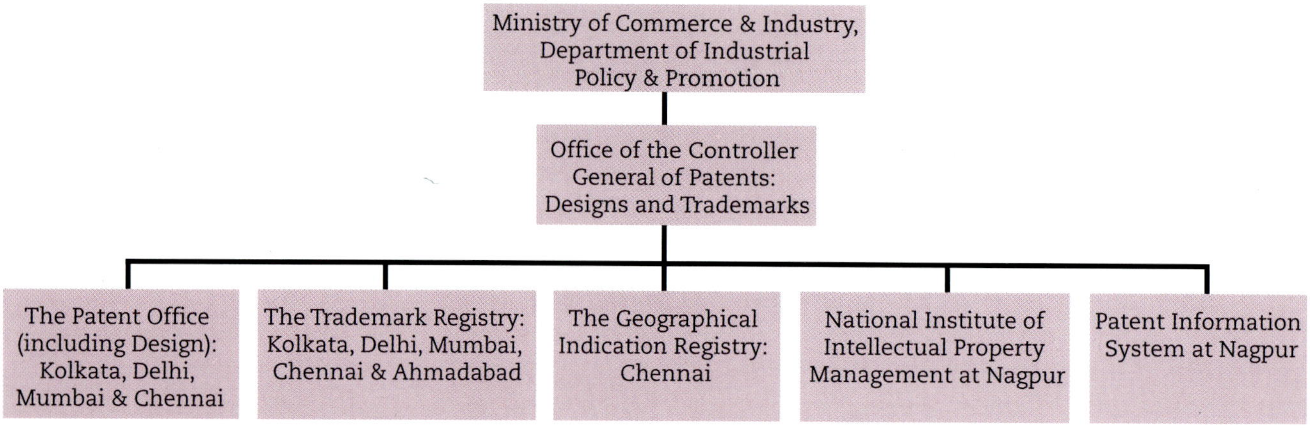

Source: Annual Report of the Office of the Controller General of Patents, Designs, Trademarks and Geographical Indication, 2010–11, India. Available at *http://ipindia.gov.in/cgpdtm/AnnualReport_English_2013_2014.pdf* (accessed on 28 March 2016).

Table 5.1

Trends of IPR Granted/Registered (2009-2014)

Year	2009-10	2010-11	2011-12	2012-13	2013-14
Patents	6168	7509	4381	4126	4227
Designs	6025	9206	6590	7252	7178
Trade Marks	67490	115472	51735	44361	67876
Geographical Indications Registered	14	29	23	21	22

Source: Annual Report of the Office of the Controller General of Patents, Designs, Trade Marks and Geographical Indication, 2013-14, India. Available at *http://ipindia.gov.in/cgpdtm/AnnualReport_English_2013_2014.pdf* (accessed on 28 March 2016).

In India, patents are concentrated in the hands of a few large companies. The top ten Indian patentees held 1008 patents in India while the top ten foreign patentees held 4331 patents. Of this, a majority of the patents were concentrated in the hands of three to four domestic and foreign companies (see Table 5.2).

In contrast to India with 1085 patent applications in the year 2013-14, the UK is the seventh largest country after the US, Japan, Germany, France, Switzerland and the Netherlands in terms of country-wise patent applications.[8]

To encourage private and foreign participation in R&D, the Indian government offers several incentives and tax concession to companies. FDI up to 100 per cent is allowed in R&D and foreign multinationals are encouraged to setup R&D centres in India.[9] Further to this, as per the Foreign Direct Investment Policy of DIPP, foreign companies that foster technology transfer are encouraged to invest in India. The Department of Electronics and Information Technology has launched a scheme, Support for International Patent Protection in Electronics and IT in 2014, to provide financial support to MSMEs and technology start-up units for international patent filing to encourage innovation and recognise the value and capabilities of global intellectual property along with capturing growth opportunities.

5.2 R&D Collaborations and International Partnerships

R&D collaboration in India takes place through several platforms such as collaborations between businesses, between different government bodies and agencies, through PPP models, between academic institutes and businesses, and between academic institutions and the government, among others.

The international collaborations are mostly in the form of bilateral cross-country R&D programmes. There are a few multi-country R&D programmes. For example, the EU's Horizon 2020 Programme can involve more than one country. Several joint R&D centres have already been established by EU Member States in India. For example, the Indo-German Science

8. For details see Annual Report of the Office of the Controller General of Patents, Designs, Trade Marks and Geographical Indication, 2013-14, India. Available at *http://ipindia.gov.in/cgpdtm/AnnualReport_English_2013_2014.pdf* (accessed on 28 March 2016).

9. For details see *http://deity.gov.in/content/industry-promotion-activities-dpl-industyactivities* (accessed on 22 September 2015) and the Consolidated FDI Policy, DIPP accessible at: *http://dipp.nic.in/English/policies/FDI_Circular_2015.pdf* (accessed on 22 September 2015).

Table 5.2

Top 10 Indian and Foreign Resident Patentees in India, 2013-14

Sl. No.	*Indian Patentees (Top among Public and Private Sector)*		*Foreign Resident Patentees*	
	Name of Organisation	*No. of Patent*	*Name of Organisation*	*No. of Patent*
1	Council of Scientific and Industrial Research	267	Qualcomm Incorporated (ICT, the US)	1062
2	Tata Consultancy Services Limited	169	Koninklijke Philips N.V. (Electronics, the Netherlands)	839
3	Defence Research & Development Organisation	116	Telefonaktie-bolaget LM Ericsson (ICT, Sweden)	386
4	Samsung R&D Institute India	84	Robert Bosch GMBH (Automotive, Germany)	375
5	Infosys Limited	83	Samsung Electronics Co. Ltd. (Electronics, South Korea)	371
6	Indian Council for Agricultural Research	71	BASF SE (Chemical, Germany)	304
7	Samsung India Software Operations Private Limited	66	Sony Corporation (Electronics, Japan)	263
8	Wipro Limited	59	General Electric Company (Electronics, the US)	260
9	Indian Institute of Technology (Collective)	59	Siemens Aktiengesells-chaft (Engineering, Germany)	249
10	Department of Biotechnology	34	Alcatel Lucent (ICT, France)	222

Source: Annual Report of the Office of the Controller General of Patents, Designs, Trade Marks and Geographical Indication, 2013–14, India. Available at *http://ipindia.gov.in/cgpdtm/AnnualReport_English_2013_2014.pdf* (accessed on 28 March 2016).

and Technology Centre, the German House for Research and Innovation (DWIH New Delhi), UKIERI, the Research Councils UK India (RCUK India) and the Innovation Centre Denmark in India, to name a few.

From the government side, DST has undertaken several initiatives to foster collaborations across different parts of the world. This includes government-to-government collaboration, government-to-industry collaboration and industry-to-industry collaboration. Depending on the form of collaborations, the source of funding R&D is determined. Bilateral cooperation includes activities such as joint research projects, scientific and ministerial missions, training programmes, access to advanced research facilities, mega projects, promoting industrial R&D and technology summits, among others.

To enhance international collaboration in knowledge-based sectors, the government has signed agreements and MoUs for collaboration in the field of science and technology with over 70 countries and is undertaking over 400 R&D projects with international collaboration.[10] Among these, a substantial number of such R&D collaborations are with the EU Member States.

India has a Science and Technology Cooperation Agreement with the UK since 1996. There are several ongoing programmes on both the sides that aim to foster R&D collaborations between India and the UK. India and the UK have bilateral R&D programmes and the companies and institutions of the two countries can participate in other multi-country programmes such as the Horizon 2020 of the EU. Among the bilateral programmes, Global Innovation and Technology Alliance (GITA) is the most prominent one. Some of the existing R&D programmes are given in Box 5.2.

The India-UK joint R&D programme, which is managed by GITA on behalf of DST, lays emphasis on commercialisation of R&D by MSMEs who may find it difficult to commercialise their innovation. About 80 per cent of the funding goes to the MSMEs in India and the UK. Companies have to identify their partners in the UK. Many companies even tie-up with academic institutions. The areas for funding are jointly decided by the Indian and the UK governments.

Other than these, funding is available for Indian entities involved in a collaborative project, which can be through one of the India specific mechanisms (such as GITA) or multilateral funding under INNO INDIGO. The latter is a European Research Area-Network with India and a successor of New Indigo Project as a part of Europe-India collaboration. This project is aimed at encouraging R&D among the small and medium enterprises. It is an implementation agency and it facilitates networking of funding organisations in India and the EU and mobilising funding from different sources. Food, agriculture and fisheries, biotechnology,

10. For details, see Department of Science and Technology website *http://www.dst.gov.in/* (accessed on 2 July 2013).

Box 5.2

Selected R&D Collaborations with the UK

Horizon 2020 of the European Union: The Horizon 2020 programme succeeds the Seventh Framework Programme (FP7) of the European Union, which aims to promote research, innovation and education to meet the Lisbon goals with a budget of EUR 80 billion (USD 89.6 billion).[1] Horizon 2020 is a collaborative R&D programme of the EU wherein Indian researchers, enterprises and institutions will be able to team up with their European partners to participate in projects under Horizon 2020.[2] Some of the key areas identified for funding under this programme include smart green and integrated transport and clean and efficient energy which has implications on food supply chain. In the case of India, funding under this programme will be available through a competitive process.

In cases where an Indian entity is about to participate in an EU project without receiving any EU funding (as this will be more frequent under Horizon 2020), the relevant Indian authorities might decide to provide funding supporting each participation (e.g., by launching matching calls for proposals). Indian participants themselves determine the sources of funding for their Indian part of the project: these may be own funds of the participating institutions, as well as funds received from Indian ministries, departments, foundations and other organisations that fund research and development activities in India.

Global Innovation and Technology Alliance (GITA): CII and DST, Government of India initiated GITA in 2007-08 to stimulate private sector's investment in R&D.[3] GITA was incorporated as a private limited company under Section 25 of the Companies Act 1956 on 29 November 2011, promoted jointly by CII and Technology Development Board of Department of Science & Technology, Government of India. CII and Technology Development Board hold 51 per cent and 49 per cent equity, respectively, in GITA. Vision of GITA is to strengthen India's innovation ecosystem through supporting and enabling technology and innovation driven enterprises. GITA was set up with an aim of providing demand-driven technology solutions through institutional and global alliances via a competitive process. Under this project, there are joint bilateral as well as multilateral programmes including those with the UK.

India-UK Programme: The India-UK Collaborative Industrial R&D Programme was launched in 2014. The programme aims to support business-led collaborative R&D projects between the Indian and UK companies including working with academic organisations from both countries. From the UK side, Innovate UK[4] is the nodal body while DST is the nodal agency in India. The programme provides grant to selected participants to build sustainable research partnerships and increase bilateral R&D collaboration contributing to economic growth and societal benefit. These programmes focus on cleantech energy, affordable healthcare, advanced manufacturing and use of ICT in the focus areas. Under this programme, up to 50 per cent of the eligible project cost is funded by the two governments.[5]

Note: 1. Currency conversion is done using *www.oanda.com* [accessed on 30 March 2016] using the exchange rate of EUR 1 = USD 1.12; 2. *http://ec.europa.eu/programmes/horizon2020/* (accessed on 22 September 2015); 3. For details see *http://gita.org.in/home.html* (accessed on 22 September 2015); 4. *https://www.gov.uk/government/organisations/innovate-uk* (accessed on 22 September 2015); 5. For detail see *http://foodlogistics.in/wp-content/uploads/2016/03/Potential_for_Developing_a_Joint_Research_and_Development_Centre.pdf.pdf* (accessed on 6 March 2016).

Source: Compiled from *https://ec.europa.eu/programmes/horizon2020/*; *http://gita.org.in/aboutus.aspx;* (accessed on 30 March 2016).

infrastructure and transport are a few selected areas where ERA-Net projects are ongoing. These could be some of the potential platforms where the government can look into R&D collaboration, depending on the needs of India, in the same way as Infect-ERA with DBT previously.

Further to these, there are several other initiatives with the UK at the government level. For instance, the UK's Department for International Development (DFID) Research and Evidence Division has several programmes wherein they fund R&D activities in India. There are several MoUs between different councils, government departments and bodies in India and the UK. For instance, the Design Council (UK) and the India Design Council entered in an MoU in November 2013 to enhance the understanding of emerging trends, design domain developments, and share design knowledge and resources through focused activities. The UK Intellectual Property Office has an IP Attaché based in the British High Commission since 2012, with an objective to develop some model contracts and guidance that could be used in UK-India collaborations.

The visit of the Indian Prime Minister to UK in November 2015 has been very beneficial for nurturing future R&D collaboration between both countries. There has been substantial success in the ongoing projects such as the Newton Bhabha fund, which has grown from less than GBP 1 million (USD 1.42 million) in 2008 to over GBP 200 million (USD 285.5 million).[11] Similarly, Innovate UK, DST and GITA, have opened up a third round of collaborative industrial R&D, making up to GBP 3.5 million (USD 4.9 million)[12] available to support novel commercial solutions in the areas of clean-tech energy, affordable healthcare and ICT related to clean-tech energy.[13] These can be applied to the food logistics sector also. New investments in R&D include multi-million pound UK India virtual centres in Clean Energy, Security and Agricultural Nitrogen, which will act as 'Centres of Excellence' and undertake joint research.[14]

Currently, there are not many partnership programmes with the UK or other countries that specifically focus on R&D in food logistics or food supply chain. However, interactions with the various stakeholders have suggested that food logistics can be considered as one of the areas for collaborative R&D between India and the UK. The survey findings are discussed below.

5.3 Primary Survey Analysis

In order to understand the views of the players engaged in R&D in food logistics and supply chain, a primary survey has been conducted covering 22 stakeholders from the industry, policymakers and government officials from India, the UK and the European Commission, among others. The discussion focuses on the scope for R&D collaborations in food supply chain and how the UK can contribute to India's R&D development.

All survey participants feel that there is scope for collaboration with the UK in R&D in food supply chain. Since most of the companies in the food supply chain in the two countries are small and MSMEs, they will benefit from government support for R&D. The UK companies have pointed out that India has a large and educated workforce, but they are worried about the slow and cumbersome patent regime. Also, they are worried about the IPR protection and they have limited knowledge of the market. Therefore, they would first try to know the market and then set up R&D centres. Cities such as Bangalore, Pune and Hyderabad are referred to as ideal places for R&D hubs in India.

11. Currency conversion is done using *www.oanda.com* (accessed on 30 March 2016) using the exchange rate of GBP 1 = USD 1.42.

12. Ibid.

13. *http://pib.nic.in/newsite/PrintRelease.aspx?relid=130408* (accessed on 6 March 2016).

14. For details see *https://www.gov.uk/government/news/joint-statement-on-the-united-kingdom-india-summit-2015* (accessed on 30 March 2016).

The survey shows that R&D in food supply chain will increase once there is corporate investment in the food processing and retail sector. A number of key global players such as Deutsche Post DHL have presence in the logistics sector of India but are yet to enter the food supply chain/food logistics. Lack of corporatisation and fragmented supply chain has limited the demand for R&D. The survey participants strongly opined that R&D will help to reduce wastage, ensure food safety, lead to reduction in transportation cost, save fuel and increase shelf life of perishable produce. Some areas were identified by the respondents for R&D collaborations. They are discussed below.

5.3.1 Packaging Technology

Survey respondents have pointed out that there is scope for R&D in India in packaging technologies such as freeze-thaw dehydration and vacuum packaging since these are used to mostly pack fresh produce. The survey has found that due to different climatic conditions, poor infrastructure and storage facilities, the UK manufacturers and retailers have to customise the packages to the Indian requirements and conditions, which needs R&D and innovation.

Another area of potential R&D collaboration is packaging design. Design innovations that provide an ease of use and transportation as well as reduce wastage are essential for turning a low price commodity into a high value product. These innovations can range from creative prints to intelligent designs for customer's ease of use; for example, PET (Polyethylene terephthalate) bottles which are curved for better grip or have handles and ketchup bottles in squeeze packs (Maggi *Pichkoo*), among others. The survey shows that DBT has already called for proposals, which are aimed at providing solutions to improve ease of transportation, extending shelf life, addressing humidity control, disease control or pest infestation, ensuring authenticity and quality package for dispensability[15] (e.g., re-sealable and tailored for specific populations, markets), and are reusable or turned into a value-added waste stream. DBT is also giving priority to eco-friendly packaging. These can be potential areas for R&D investment and collaborations.

Survey respondents have pointed out that the demand for eco-friendly packaging is growing in India. Companies such as Uflex Limited have come up with various methods of sustainable packaging such as usage of bio-plastics. Tetra Pak India Private

15. For details see, Department of Biotechnology, Innovate UK and Research Councils UK, 2015.

Limited is working towards reducing/replacing the aluminium in their aseptic packaging because of the environmental concerns and is looking at eco-friendly options. There is scope for collaboration with the UK in R&D and innovation related to eco-friendly packaging. India needs R&D in packaging materials R&D so that food safety standards are ensured and health of the consumers is protected.

5.3.2 Clean Technology

It is found during the survey that there is scope for R&D collaboration in clean technology. This is an area where there is significant government funding in the UK and there are funds available through other cross-country research programmes such as Horizon 2020. Clean technology is a priority area for the UK funding agency in their research programme for India.

There is scope for collaborative research in use of solar and alternative fuel for cold storages and pack-houses, battery operated vehicles and development of charging stations for the same, light weight containers for transportation, multi-chambered refrigerated vehicles, etc. Some companies such as Bharat Solar Energy are already providing solutions for solar powered reefer trucks in India.[16] In the United States, Carrier Transicold has developed a technology to harness energy from solar panels into the refrigeration units. These 'Thin-Film Flexible Solar Panels' can be easily installed on the roofs of trailers, truck bodies and refrigerated rail cars. These technologies are yet to be adopted in India. There is need for R&D to reduce the cost of alternative fuel and to customise the global technologies to Indian road and climatic conditions.

It is further pointed out during the survey that clean technology can be sourced from recycling of organic waste products such as timber waste, forest debris, crops, manure, etc. There is need for research to see how such biomass-based alternative sources of energy can be used in food supply chain.

There is scope for R&D in another niche area, Liquid Air Refrigeration, which involves harnessing liquid air to deliver zero emission power cooling to create global food chains. This kind of technological investment is being made by Dearman Engines,[17] a UK-based company. Considering that India has the potential and need for developing cold-chain facilities, the company has proposed to make investments in India.

In some areas, technology is evolving in developed countries including the UK (for example, automatic refrigerated vehicles without drivers). Once these technologies are tested in markets such as the UK, they can be tried out in India. However, given the road conditions and traffic, many survey participants have pointed out that these technologies may not be successful in India.

A niche area where there is scope for R&D is related to utilisation of stranded cold from liquified natural gas (LNG) terminals at ports for generating power. This can be used for various purposes including the provision of electricity to local cold storages as well as reefer trucks through cryogenic engines. This has also been pointed out by NCCD and is reiterated during our survey. The concept of stranded cold involves re-gasification of liquid natural gas, which not only provides clean energy with zero carbon dioxide but also generates huge amount of power. There are some proposed LNG terminals states such as Odisha, Karnataka, Gujarat, Andhra Pradesh, Tamil Nadu and West Bengal in India.

5.3.3 R&D in Product Handing

There is scope for joint R&D between the India and UK companies in product handing, especially perishables to increase their shelf life and reduce wastage. There is need for R&D in India to preserve food safety and reduce adulteration due to mishandling. Automatic product handling and inventory management using IT are areas where India needs R&D.

5.3.4 R&D in Product Transportation

The need for efficient and reliable cooling technology for urban deliveries is rapidly increasing. During the survey, Carrier Transicold has pointed out that they have launched the 'Citimax' range of light commercial vehicle and truck refrigeration units in India, aiming at enhancing the short haul transportation component of the supply chain. The company claims that the special refrigeration equipment helps in preserving the temperature by quick pre-cooling and rapid recovery after each door opening. The "Citimax" range is capable of reaching the set point 20 per cent faster than previous direct-drive units, enabling reduced load times. There is scope for R&D for vehicles for short haul deliveries.

With the implementation of dedicated freight corridors in India, there will be demand for refrigerated

16. For details, please see *http://www.bharatsolarenergy.com/* (accessed on 10 March 2016).

17. For details see, *http://www.dearman.co.uk/#!cold-and-power/cjg4* and *http://www.dearman.co.uk/#!Entrepreneur-India-Cold-chain-investment-in-India-to-reach-15-billion-in-next-5-years-Report/ccrp/551430ff0cf215f35a1bcdc9* (accessed on 10 March 2016).

containers which will be transported by railways. This will be an area for R&D and innovation.

5.4.4 Other Areas

To improve the efficiency of the food supply chain, India needs to have service stations and check posts of global standards. There is need for R&D to development service stations and check posts of international standards but customised to Indian requirements.

Overall, the survey shows that there are several areas for R&D and collaboration between Indian companies, institutes, academicians and their UK counterparts. The government of the two countries are already support joint R&D programmes. However, the funds allocated may not be enough given the wide range of research areas and paucity of private investment in research in India. Further, technologies developed in the UK may have to be customised for India and hence there is need for innovation. Success of collaborative R&D will depend on the removal of barriers to R&D, which are discussed in the next section.

Section

6

Barriers Faced in the Food Supply Chain

The previous sections of the report have highlighted that there are several opportunities for investments by the UK companies and institutions in different sub-sectors of the food supply chain. Given the complementarities between businesses and institutions of the two countries, such investments will be mutually beneficial. However, the survey has found that the presence of the UK companies and institutions in the food supply chain of India is limited in spite of liberalisation and the reforms that India has undertaken in the recent years. In fact, the presence of the private corporate sector in India's food supply chain is low. This is due to a number of barriers, which are also restricting the entry and operations of the UK businesses. Some of these are general barriers that are applicable to all companies (foreign and domestic) across all verticals. There are some sector specific barriers. This section discusses both general and sector specific barriers in sub-sections 6.1 and 6.2, respectively. The sector specific barriers focus on five areas, namely storage and warehousing, cold-chains, packaging technology, skills development and R&D in food logistics. The analysis in this section is largely based on the primary survey findings and has been substantiated by secondary information, wherever it is available.

6.1 General Barriers

India continues to be a difficult market for businesses. This is reflected by the low ranking of the country in World Bank's Ease of Doing Business indicators. In 2014, India was ranked 134th among 189 countries in terms of ease of doing business. India's rank fell down to 142 in 2015 and improved to 130th in 2016. Compared to 2014, although there has been a slight improvement in the ranking of the country but the performance is not consistent. Compared to this, the UK ranks 6th in 2016 in terms of ease of doing business. Detailed ranking for each indicator considered while calculating the ease of doing business is given in Figure 6.1. As illustrated in the figure, it is much tougher to start a business or get permits and clearances, register a property or pay taxes, among other things in India as compared to the UK.[1]

In November 2015, a survey was conducted by UKIBC[2] on 'Doing Business in India'. Although this survey does not specifically focus on food supply chain, it tries to capture the perspective of the UK companies on India's business environment. The findings of our survey are similar to the UKIBC survey. Both the surveys show that legal and regulatory impediment are the biggest barriers faced by the UK businesses in India. Around 67.09 per cent of the respondents in the UKIBC survey considered this as the biggest impediments.

Figure 6.1

Comparative Performance of India and the UK on the Ease of Doing Business Indicators in 2016

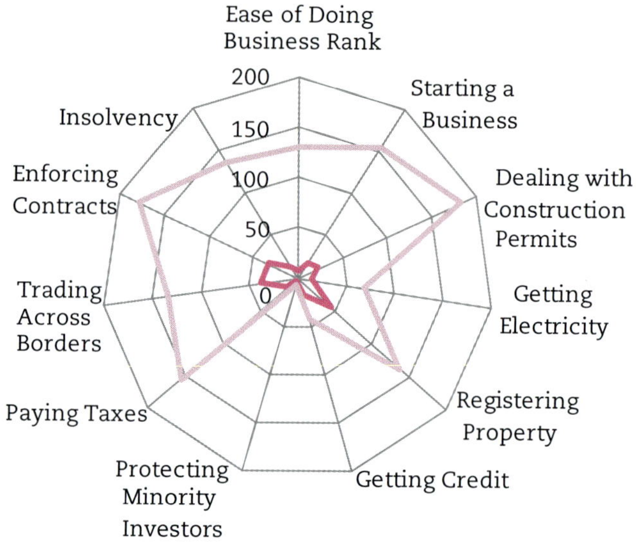

Note: The closer a country is to the centre, the better is its rank on that indicator.
Source: Extracted from Ease of Doing Business Indicators of the World Bank see *http://www.doingbusiness.org/rankings* (accessed on 30 March 2016).

A number of operational barriers in India stem from the fact that India has a quasi-federal governance structure and there is division of regulatory responsibilities between multiple ministries and departments of the central and state governments. As a result, there are multiple regulatory agencies and a large number of regulations affecting the food supply chain. Each state has its own regulatory framework. Multiplicity of regulation acts as a deterrent to foreign investment and ease of doing business. The survey points out that India does not operate like a single market and it is difficult to set up food supply chain across multiple states.

Further, state-level policies are crucial in food supply chain as areas such as retail and agriculture are within the jurisdiction of the state governments. For instance, sourcing conditions through the Agricultural Produce and Marketing Committee Act and inter-state

1. For details on India's ranking on the Ease of Doing Business Indicators of the World Bank see *http://www.doingbusiness.org/rankings* (accessed on 16 March 2016).
2. For details see *https://www.ukibc.com/reports/ease-of-doing-business-in-india-the-uk-perspective-november-2015/* (accessed on 17 March 2016). The survey is based on information collected from over 100 UK businesses operating in India.

restrictions on movement of cargo are imposed by the states. States vary in their approach to liberalisation of retail and in allowing foreign and corporate sector to work directly with the farmers. Moreover, the number of approvals required, the process of filing for the approvals and time taken for the approvals to be cleared vary across states. States with greater ease of doing business attract investment. In September 2015, DIPP along with the World Bank, KPMG, CII and FICCI released a report assessing the state-wise implementation of business reforms.[3] Based on the comparative performance of each state, the ranking of different Indian states is placed in Table 6.1. As per the ranking, in 2015, Gujarat was the best performing Indian state while Arunachal Pradesh was the worst.

Table 6.1

State Ranking Based on the Implementation of Reforms in 2015

Rank	*State/Union Territory*	*Rank*	*State/Union Territory*
1	Gujarat	17	Himachal Pradesh
2	Andhra Pradesh	18	Kerala
3	Jharkhand	19	Goa
4	Chhattisgarh	20	Puducherry
5	Madhya Pradesh	21	Bihar
6	Rajasthan	22	Assam
7	Odisha	23	Uttarakhand
8	Maharashtra	24	Chandigarh
9	Karnataka	25	Andaman and Nicobar Islands
10	Uttar Pradesh	26	Tripura
11	West Bengal	27	Sikkim
12	Tamil Nadu	28	Mizoram
13	Telangana	29	Jammu and Kashmir
14	Haryana	30	Meghalaya
15	Delhi	31	Nagaland
16	Punjab	32	Arunachal Pradesh

Source: Compiled from Assessment of State Implementation of Business Reforms, Section 2.3.1, page 10. Available at http://indiainbusiness.nic.in/newdesign/upload/StateAssessmentReport_14September2015.pdf (accessed on 30 March 2016).

States compete among themselves to get foreign investment. However, until policies are streamlined throughout the country, it is unlikely to result in improved investment climate and this will act as a deterrent to the businesses interested in establishing pan-India operations.

Another key issue is that of high and multi-layered taxes. India has a much higher corporate tax than most ASEAN countries such as Singapore and Thailand, making India uncompetitive to them.[4] This was also highlighted in the UKIBC survey. Although the Union Budget 2015-16 promised to reduce the corporate taxes, this has not happened for the larger companies in the Union Budget of 2016-17. The corporate tax rate in India is more than 30 per cent and is coupled with additional charges. The government also imposes a number of cess on the corporate sector which further increases the tax burden. In addition, there are multiple taxes that come into play with the movement of goods from one state to another. In fact, there are three layers of taxes—one at the centre such as Central Sales Tax, at the state-level such as Value Added Tax (VAT) and also at the municipal level such as Octroi in Mumbai, Maharashtra. Due to the multi-layered taxes, the costs of operations increase. Multi-layered taxes and variation of taxes across states make it difficult to have a pan-India pricing and hub-and-spoke model of operation.

Despite a series of reforms related to the FDI liberalisation, the presence of the UK businesses in India is limited. Large foreign multi-brand retailers such a Wal-Mart Stores Incorporated and Tesco Plc are present in India only as wholesale cash and carry operators. None of the UK companies have entered the food retail business. This is mainly due to the restrictions on FDI in multi-brand retail. A number of survey participants have pointed out that UK companies in the food supply chain usually follow their retailers and manufacturers to enter new markets. The low presence of global multinationals and domestic corporate players in food manufacturing and retailing have led to the low presence of the UK companies in food supply chain sector of India. Most companies are waiting for FDI liberalisation across the entire supply chain. A number of companies have expressed concerns about the inability of Tesco Plc to speed up investments in India. Most of the UK businesses are in the wait-and-watch mode and they are closely watching the success of other UK businesses that have entered or are planning to enter the Indian market.

A number of survey respondents have pointed out that the pace of reforms is considerably slow in the country—for instance, the GST is yet to be implemented and businesses continue to face multilayered

3. The report is available at *http://indiainbusiness.nic.in/newdesign/upload/StateAssessmentReport_14September2015.pdf* (accessed on 30 March 2016).

4. For details on comparative tax rates see *http://www2.deloitte.com/content/dam/Deloitte/global/Documents/Tax/dttl-tax-corporate-tax-rates-2015.pdf* (accessed on 17 March 2016).

taxes. The government has not been successful in addressing the issues related to compensation under the land acquisition regulation. Compensations under the Right to Fair Compensation and Transparency in Land Acquisition, Rehabilitation and Resettlement (Amendment) Bill, 2015 are prime concerns for companies that are part of large projects such as those planning to develop cold-chains along economic corridors. In the case of manufacturing, there are issues such as outdated labour laws in which the reforms are pending. The present government does not have a majority in the Upper House of the Parliament or Rajya Sabha and therefore is unable to push forward the reforms. Some reforms, such as those related to liberalisation of FDI in multi-brand retail,are pending due to political reasons. Further, the government's international trade negotiations, especially the India-EU Broad-based Trade and Investment Agreement (BTIA), are moving at a slow pace. The UK companies have pointed out that commitment in the trade agreement would have ensured operational certainty. They have raised concerns about frequent changes in policies in India. Many of them are contemplating entry into the Indian market through ASEAN countries like Singapore for more conducive trade and investment agreements.

There are several infrastructure-related issues. These are as follows:

1. The supply chain in India continues to be fragmented with multiple small players. The government policies and incentives support smaller players, which further leads to fragmented supply chain. In 2015, 98.4 per cent of the food and grocery sector was in the unorganised sector.[5] As a result, traceability continues to be an issue. Moreover, the handling of agricultural commodities is done in a labour intensive and unorganised manner leading to low demand of sophisticated infrastructure.

2. Second, support infrastructure such as water, power and roads poses one of the most critical challenges in the development of food supply chain India. The rural road network is about 2.7 million kilometres long but almost a million kilometres do not meet technical standards required (Ministry of Agriculture 2008).[6] Poor roadways lead to damages to the perishables and cause premature food loss in the supply chain. Similarly, the lack of reliable and affordable electricity has created a crucial bottleneck in the development process. Due to poor quality of power supply and frequent power cuts, companies have to make their captive power arrangements such as diesel gensets which add to the costs.

3. Third, for warehouses and cold storages, ripening chambers and pack-houses, it is important to have the land at the right location (close to the agriculture areas, ports, metro cities, etc.). The private developers are facing several issues with respect to land. The cost of land near prime locations such as vicinity of metro cities and ports is very high. In many states, it is difficult to convert agricultural land into other activities such as development of warehouses and cold-chains. Land is a state subject and there are significant variations across states in terms of their approach towards cold-chain development. Even where land is available with State Industrial Development Corporations in some states, it takes over 6-8 months to get clearances for the land. The delay and process in acquiring change in land use have a negative impact on the cold-chain development.

4. Fourth, the financial infrastructure in the country is also poor. A majority of the operators in the sector are small and medium enterprises and they often face shortages of funds. The cost of borrowing is high, which discourages modernisation and technological adaptation.

Another barrier pointed out during the survey is corruption and lack of transparency in the system. This is particularly true at the state level. Based on a survey of 168 countries, Transparency International releases the Corruption Perceptions Index.[7] In 2015, India was ranked 76th among 168 countries while the UK was ranked 10th. The UKIBC survey also highlights corruption as a key barrier for the UK businesses.

It is pointed out in the survey that the legal framework in India is weak and so is the dispute settlement mechanism. It takes a long time and entails high cost to settle disputes in India. The UKIBC survey has similar findings. The two surveys show that although there has been some change in the business environment in the past two years, there is need for more changes.

5. Images Multimedia Private Limited (2015).
6. Ministry of Agriculture (2008).
7. For details see *http://www.transparency.org/cpi2015#results-table* (accessed on 17 March 2016).

The survey participants have raised concerns about the level of awareness and knowledge among the lower level officials of the central and state governments. The officials of the central government change frequently and this adds to the problems faced by foreign businesses. The companies raise several concerns with respect to the e-business portal and argue that there is need for greater transparency and clarity on self-certification and processes such as single window clearances. Also, queries and grievances are raised by government departments in a sporadic manner and are not addressed within a fixed time frame.

Agriculture and processed food is a sensitive sector in India and the country imposes high tariffs and other trade restrictions. The import duties on a number of items are high. In its trade agreements with trading partners such as the ASEAN, India made commitments to lower import duties on a number of products in a phased manner which adversely affected the UK companies which were exporting to India. The UK companies are now at a disadvantage vis a vis companies from other countries with which India has a trade agreement. The high tariff discourages foreign investors from establishing value chains in the country. A number of UK companies have pointed out that they would like to investment in FTWZs and SEZs. However, sales from SEZs in India to the domestic tariff area faces a high autonomous tariff while the same product from countries such as Thailand with which India has a trade agreement faces a lower tariff. Thus, companies find it easier to sell products from their manufacturing facilities in countries such as Thailand to India than manufacturing in Indian SEZs. Further, a number of subsidies given to the manufacturing sector in India, especially the export linked subsides, can be actionable under the WTO. Therefore, the UK food processing companies are not keen to invest in India only for the tax incentives and subsidies.

In addition to these tariff discrepancies, the custom procedures in India are cumbersome. The interpretation of the policy by customs varies across ports. There are licencing, labelling and packaging conditions along with other standards laid down by FSSAI that often change without prior indication. This adversely affects international businesses. A number of UK companies have pointed out that if they manufacture and import the product from India, they face food safety and standards issue in the UK. The differences in food safety standards and its implementation adversely impact the setting up of cross country food supply chain.

Due to the presence of small and fragmented players in the food supply chain, the technology adaptation of this sector is low. As discussed earlier, most of the warehouses and storage facilities in India are manual. The survey participants have pointed out that the food supply chain in India today is as it was in the UK in the mid-1980s. It is therefore difficult for the UK companies to bring in the latest technology because they have to first customise the technology to the market, weather conditions, available infrastructure, etc. This entails cost. The corporate sector in India faces stiff competition from the non-corporate sector and the latter can pay lower taxes and get several benefits from the government. The non-corporate sector is highly price-competitive and India is a price-sensitive market. Further, due to the lack of corporatisation in food processing and retailing sector, food supply chain companies have limited corporate clients.

Even though electronic business (commonly called "e-biz") portals are being set up by the governments at the centre and states, most of the UK companies are either not aware of the portal or have difficulties in using it. Most UK business in the sector are small and medium size operators. They lack knowledge about the Indian market and are worried about selecting the right partner. The UK companies, Indian companies and other foreign companies have pointed out that there is shortage of data on the available infrastructure in India. The data on the growth of the sector and its growth projections are provided by different consultancy organisation and the data vary widely. Even the data on wastage in the food supply chain provided by NCCD and MoFPI are widely different. While there are issues common to all sectors in the food supply chain, the survey throws light on several sector specific issues. There are discussed in the next sub-section.

6.2 Sector-Specific Barriers

The different sectors in the food supply chain in India face issues unique to these sectors. While some of these issues are related to the market and operational structure, others stem out of the policies and quasi-federal nature of governance in India. These are summarised below.

6.2.1 Storage and Warehousing Sector

- The storage and warehouses sector in India is dominated by the government or government agencies and the UK companies are more willing to work with the private sector. In the UK, the warehouse sector is completely privatised. Some companies raise concerns about the government procurement norms and warehouse rates.

- The storage and warehousing sector in India is one of the most fragmented sectors in the food supply chain. Most of the owners have 1-2 storages. The warehouses in India are small, and are designed to meet the basic requirements set by WDRA without any automation or use of technology. The sporadic development of warehouses, which offer highly competitive rates for the users, prevent development of modern warehouses and penetration of technology.
- The UK companies and associations express their difficulties in identifying the right partner.
- There is inconsistency in food safety and health standards across states.

6.2.2 Cold-chain

- High energy costs in India, along with frequent power cuts, lead to a higher cost of investment and operating expenses in the cold-chain. This is rated as the most important barrier for cold storages and pack-houses. According to a report, operating costs for the cold storages business in India are approximately INR 70-90 per cubic ft. per year as against INR 40 per cubic ft. per year in developed countries. Further, the report states that energy costs alone make up about 30 per cent of the total expenses for the cold storage industry in India compared to 10 per cent in the west.[8] On top of that, frequent power cuts lead to cold-chain players to look for back-up systems/ alternate sources which are generally diesel fuel driven with associated costs, which lead to increase in prices of cold storage and the reefer transportation.
- The market is fragmented and price sensitive. It is very difficult to develop an integrated cold-chain from farm-to-fork for the domestic market. Even the corporate sector competes on price and works on thin profit margins.
- Investments in cold-chains in India have a long gestation period. Cold-chains require heavy initial investment and due to the fragmented nature of the sector with various policy issues, the time taken to break-even on investment is about 5-7 years according to the survey respondents. Most of the companies operating in the cold-chain are capital intensive (cost of real estate and refrigeration equipments) and the Return on Capital Employed (ROCE) is low. Major part of the funding in the cold-chain industry is done through debt funding which results in heavy interest expenses. This has a negative impact on the net profit generated by the cold-chain player.
- Without the implementation of the GST, companies will not be able to set up integrated cold-chain networks.
- There is no information available on the total number of cold storages, etc., and their location and capacity. NCCD only has information of cold storages build with subsidies and/or grants.
- It is extremely difficult to get trained drivers for refrigerated vehicles and trained personnel at the floor of the cold storages and pack-houses. There is a lack of sensitivity towards perishables being transported since the drivers may not be aware or they may be aware but still they turn off the refrigeration units in order to save fuel. This leads to products getting spoiled/degradation of quality. A lot of produce is wasted due to manhandling in the cold-chain. Further, many respondents have mentioned that it is difficult to get good drivers because there are not enough facilities for the drivers while they drive on the highways. Indian highways lack basic requirements like public facilities, vehicle service facilities in case of a breakdown, safe places to park the vehicles, etc.
- The cold-chain sector is heavily reliant on fossil fuels for running the refrigeration units in both cold storages and reefers. There is a shortage of technology related to energy optimisation, automation systems, data recorders and other sensors which are important for optimisation of cold storage operations. Unlike developed countries, government incentives are not linked to the best technology or clean technology. Hence, there is lower motivation

---

8. *http://www.onicra.com/images/pdf/publications/coldchainindustryreportjune2014.pdf* (accessed on 18 March 2016).

to use better technology and alternative fuel. Further alternative and renewable technology is costly as polluting fuel like diesel is subsidised in India.

- For efficient operation and better productivity, the cold-chain sector should be integrated. Although, a number of government bodies at the centre and state offer several incentives to the cold-chain sector, these are given in a sporadic manner without taking into consideration the requirement of the sector. For example, until recently, most of the incentives were primarily directed towards creation of cold storage facilities. This has led to over investment by private players in cold storage sector while other sub-sectors such as reefer vehicles and pack-houses have investment shortfalls. Piecemeal investment has also led to fragmented development in the sector. Moreover, small quantum of grants has led to investment by traders and middlemen rather than companies with proven experience in development of cold-chains. Moreover, due to the quasi-federal governance structure, different states have different rules, taxes, subsidies and schemes related to cold-chain which prevent an integrated development of infrastructure across multiple states. While NCCD has set up guidelines for cold-chains, MoFPI has its own requirements for giving grants for development of cold-chains. This shows lack of coordination between government departments.

6.2.3 Packaging Technology

- Packaging industry, being an ancillary industry, requires supporting infrastructure for modern packaging technologies. For example, food products packaged using freeze-thaw technology would require investments in the form of cold storage infrastructure. In the absence of the required infrastructure, potential investments in modern packaging cannot happen. Further, if a sophisticated packaging technology has to be implemented in the pack-houses or at the farm, it requires continuous supply of quality power. There are power outages and erratic supply, which make it difficult to use the machinery in the fields.

- The UK packaging companies point out that they face problems in finding the right partner. A local partner would help them identify the market opportunities and the local product requirements. However, they are worried about sharing information about the technology and best management practices with the local partner without knowing the partner.

- High taxes on processed food vis-à-vis fresh produce restrict the growth of packaging industry.

- There exist cultural differences between the UK and India in terms of business operations as well as customer tastes. For example, Indian consumers prefer fresh products vis-à-vis packaged product while in the UK, packaged products are preferred and cheaper than fresh food products.

- Although the Indian government has focused on a cluster-based approach to developing manufacturing industry, the schemes such the Mega Food Park Scheme offer benefits mainly to developers and not to the users or the manufacturing units.

- The India-EU BTIA negotiations have been ongoing since 2007. Unless the negotiations are concluded, companies in the EU including the UK will be at a disadvantage vis-à-vis companies in the countries with which India has signed a BTIA. For example, India's trade with the ASEAN countries and East Asia (Japan, Korea, etc.) in agriculture and processed food, especially imports, have increased. Packaging companies also prefer to source raw materials and machineries from countries with which India has trade agreements to get the benefits of lower tariffs.

- Companies in the corporate sector face stiff price competition from the informal/non-corporate sector. Food processing sector as well as food retail sector is underdeveloped. None of the global players such as Tesco Plc and Wal-Mart Stores, Inc. have entered Indian retail sector in a big way. Thus, the variety of food products is limited. The absence of a wide range of food products discourages packaging companies to enter Indian markets.

6.2.4 Skill Development

- The approach to skill development is different in India and the UK. The survey shows that vocational training in the UK is encouraged at the school level and the attitudes towards vocational courses are more positive in the UK as compared to India. Skill development institutions in India point out that the trainees enrolled for vocational courses usually belong to the middle and lower income groups and the motivation for obtaining vocational training often arises due to financial constraints. This is in contrast with the UK, where the trainees opt into the vocational courses as a matter of choice rather than compulsion.

- The UK and Indian food supply chain logistics sectors are different in terms of technological capabilities, level of development and business models. The UK has a highly sophisticated food supply chain whereas in India, the food supply chain is evolving technologically and some of the technologies that are widely used in the UK are yet to enter the Indian market. Therefore, the food supply chain logistics skill development courses and training programmes offered in the UK cannot be directly replicated in India and the courses and training modules have to be customised according to the requirements of the Indian industry. This would entail costs. Companies would not be willing to incur these costs unless there is sufficient demand for such training from students and companies. Further, the courses may have to be designed in local languages which would further add to the costs.

- Although the food supply chain logistics market is growing presently, survey participants express concerns regarding the future growth of the sector. There are restrictions on FDI in retail in India and these restrictions lower the incentives of global food and grocery retailers, their manufacturers and suppliers and the supply chain agents to enter India. With the low presence of foreign retailers, supply chain agents and small and mid-sized UK manufacturers are not very keen to enter the Indian market. As a result, the current demand for skilled personnel may not be sustainable in the long run.

- Survey participants from the UK have pointed out that they prefer to collaborate with private players in order to have autonomy in their operations. In the segment of skill and training too, there is a large presence of government institutions in India and the UK companies and institutes have raised concerns about administrative independence and autonomy.

- The Indian industry associations and companies have raised concerns about the high course fees in the UK. They have also highlighted the high costs of sophisticated tools and equipment that would be required for the courses, in case they enter into collaborations with the UK. Skill development in areas such as warehousing and cold-chain can lead to significant capital costs in the form of equipment to provide hands-on training such as forklifts, reefer trucks, among others. Moreover, there can be challenges related to obtaining industry sponsorship for courses or funding support to establish a training centre.

- In India vocational courses are not well-connected to the universities unlike the UK. Further there are wide variations in standards across Indian training institutes such as ITIs.

- Indian non-corporate players in the food supply chain logistics do not want to invest in formal skill development. Both corporate and non-corporate sectors prefer contractual labour. This is primarily due to the rigid labour laws which encourage even the corporate sector to employ contractual labour rather than permanent employees. This reduces the incentive to invest in training and skill development.

- There are barriers to movement of people between India and the UK. Although business visas have now become much simpler in India, there are high visa fees in the UK and the UK does not offer visa-on-arrival to Indians. India has extended the facility of e-visa to British nationals, which makes it convenient for the UK nationals to obtain an Indian visa. However, Indians travelling to the UK cannot avail this facility. The time period for a short-term visa application for the UK is 5-10 days through the normal route, while a student visa takes almost three weeks. Unless the visa process is faster and flexible, short-term movement of trainees and trainers may be difficult.

- A number of participants have pointed out that since supply chain skill development centres offer multiplicity of courses catering to different sectors such as warehousing, packaging and cold-chains, it is extremely difficult to align these different courses into a common certification framework, which is recognised in both the UK and India.

6.2.5 Research and Development

- In India, the R&D ecosystem is a major barrier to R&D collaboration between India and the UK. Patent protection is a challenge in India and this has implications on foreign collaborations. Unlike other countries, India does not allow ever greening or extension of patents. The Indian IPR regulations are different from the regulations in developed countries such as the US and the UK and the filing process is time-consuming. The legal process is slow and there are concerns about patent infringements. Further, the patent system does not cover software which is copyright in India.

- In India, majority of the R&D takes place in sectors such as defence, space, and atomic energy, which are promoted by the government. There is hardly any government incentive or scheme for R&D specific to the food supply chain logistics. Even though there are multiple schemes and concessions, the amount allotted to R&D in each of these is small and there is a long bureaucratic process for approvals.

- The funding under the joint India-UK initiatives through GITA is also low, and till date food supply chain logistics has not been identified as a priority sector for funding. Further, while the programme requires joint partnership between the Indian and UK companies, the criteria for evaluation are different in India and the UK. This is a major issue faced by the companies applying jointly for the funds.

- Only a few Indian companies have the scale and the finances to invest in R&D. The government does not provide any incentives to the private sector to invest in R&D. On the contrary, they face high corporate taxes and multiple cess which discourages investment in R&D.

- The network of academic institute, research organisation and industry is weak. It is difficult to get the R&D commercialised. Less than 10 per cent of India's R&D is for commercial use.

- One of the biggest problems is the way R&D is defined by the Income Tax Act, 1961 in India. It does not take in account non-tangible research work. This implies that services such as software cannot be patented in India; they are eligible for a copyright. As a result, the incentives and benefits available for innovation and R&D in the Income Tax Act, 1962 are not applicable for these.

- Human resource mobility is a key factor for cross-country R&D programmes. There are several visa-related issues between India and the UK and other European countries. The UK visa regime has become more stringent overtime and visa fees are high. Since mobility of people is a challenge, there is an adverse impact on R&D collaboration between the two countries.

- The level of awareness of the UK companies about new initiatives such as 'Start-up Initiative' is low.

- Unlike countries such as China which have high technology zones which are a form of SEZs with world-class infrastructure, patenting and other R&D facilities in one cluster, India does not have any high technology or state-of-the-art R&D cluster.

- Companies also raise concerns about the variety of education and skill levels of India. The Indian technical institutes have wide variation in their education standards and quality of teaching and students. There is a shortage of scientific personnel with doctorate or post-doctorate degree.

The above analysis highlights that there are several barriers faced by the UK businesses in establishing presence in the food logistics sector in India or entering in collaboration for skill development and R&D. While some of these issues are regulatory and fiscal issues, others are related to differences in the two markets in terms of levels of developments and the poor quality of infrastructure in India. These barriers, if addressed, will help in enhancing investments and collaborations between India and the UK. The next section presents some recommendations and the way forward.

Section 7

Recommendations and the Way Forward

The food logistics sector in India is poised for growth. In the Union Budget of 2016-17, the Finance Minister announced several incentives and reforms applicable to food businesses. Considering the large size of the Indian market, there is a strong interest among the UK businesses in the Indian food supply chain sector. This gathered momentum after the Indian Prime Minister's visit to the UK in November 2015. Several policy reforms were announced at that time related to FDI, clearly indicating the interest of the Indian government towards attracting foreign investment. During the survey, the UK companies, business councils and associations agreed that it is the right time for the UK companies to have an aggressive market entry strategy for India.

In this context, it is worth mentioning that agriculture and the entire food supply chain is a priority sector for both the Indian and the UK governments. The Indian government wants to reduce wastages in the supply chain while the UK government wants to increase the country's exports of agricultural produce to India and diversify the export base for agriculture exports. The UK government is encouraging the UK companies to invest in India while the Indian government is trying to attract FDI through 'Make in India', 'Start-up India' and other similar initiatives. The Indian government is also keen to implement the WTO's Agreement on Trade Facilitation and undertake business facilitation measures so that it reduces the cost of doing business. The UK can be a key partner in implementing the trade facilitation measures. Precisely, the UK companies can help India to set up state-of-the-art modern storage and warehousing facilities and cold-chains. The UK companies can participate in the 'Skill India' initiatives to upgrade the skill levels of manpower in the supply chain. Investment by the UK companies in packaging technologies will help modernise the sector, reduce wastages and increase shelf life of produce.

The previous sections have identified a number of areas where there is scope for mutually beneficial India-UK collaborations and inflow of investments from the UK. However, the presence of the UK and other foreign companies in India's food supply chain is limited. This is due to several barriers, which have been listed in Section 6. These include policy and regulatory hurdles, infrastructure bottlenecks, fiscal barriers, fragmented supply chain with dominance of informal sector, low level of technology adaptation and lack of knowledge of the market and issues in identifying the right partners, among others. While some of these barriers require domestic reforms in India, others can be addressed by UKTI and UKIBC or through greater government-to-government collaborations and collaboration between the business councils of the two countries. This section highlights these reforms in four sub-sections. The first sub-section presents the reforms that can be undertaken by India. The second sub-section dwells into the sector-specific reforms. The third sub-section points out what UKTI and UKIBC do and the last sub-section presents areas of intergovernmental and business-to-business cooperation.

7.1 What India Can Do?

It is important to note that a number of regulatory issues that came up during the survey are inter-connected and linked to three key issues: a) regulatory barriers, b) slow pace of reforms and piecemeal reforms and c) lack of transparency in governance. All of these contribute to poor ranking in the ease of doing business and creating operational uncertainties for international businesses. For instance, issues with land acquisition, retail liberalisation and multi-layer taxes are unresolved for many years due to the slow pace of reforms. Keeping in view the business concerns, the Indian government initiated land reforms through the Right to Fair Compensation and Transparency in Land Acquisition, Rehabilitation and Resettlement (LARR) Act, 2013. The LARR Act, 2013 outlines the process to be followed when land is acquired for projects involving "agro-processing, supply of inputs to agriculture, warehousing, cold storage facilities, marketing infrastructure for agriculture and allied activities such as dairy, fisheries, and meat processing, set up or owned by the appropriate Government or by a farmers' cooperative or by an institution set up under a statute" (see Page 2, Section 2.b.ii of the Act).[1] However, an amendment to the Act, The Right to Fair Compensation and Transparency in Land Acquisition, Rehabilitation and Resettlement (Amendment) Bill, 2015 was introduced in the Lok Sabha in 2015 and is yet to be presented and cleared in the Rajya Sabha. Unless this is passed, the provisions of the Act are unclear and ambiguous.

Unless FDI is allowed in multi-brand retail and the rigid conditions are removed, the food supply chain sector will not get the desired foreign investments. Global retailers play a key role in promoting agriculture exports and setting up of the food supply chain. During the survey, a number of UK companies in food logistics business have pointed out that they will enter the Indian market only when global retailers and small and mid-sized manufacturers enter the market. They have also clearly stated that they will not set up their

1. For details see *http://indiacode.nic.in/acts-in-pdf/302013.pdf* (accessed on 22 March 2016)

sourcing network from India unless they are allowed to cater to the domestic market. The retail policy should not impose restrictions on store and non-store retail formats. Some of the UK food manufacturers have or are planning to set up manufacturing hubs in ASEAN countries such as Thailand and export the products to India through the ASEAN free trade agreement (FTA). These products will then reach the Indian consumers through store (both corporate and non-corporate) and non-store retail formats. However, India will not get the desired investment in manufacturing unless the country allows global companies access to distribution and retail. It is important for the government to know that global retailers cannot change their business models to meet the conditions imposed on FDI in retail. As India competes with other countries to get FDI it should also have similar FDI policies.

The GST Bill, 2014 aims to create a harmonised tax system in the country by streamlining the tax structure and removing cascading taxes. This bill was introduced as an amendment to the Constitution and is still pending in the Parliament. A number of survey respondents have pointed out that GST is likely to have a positive impact. In anticipation of this Bill, businesses have stalled their entry-plans to the Indian market. It is urgent to implement GST since apart from creating a unified market across India, GST will help make India's manufacturing competitive by cutting high logistics costs. While GST will help address some of the interstate differences in taxes, others such as Octroi may continue. It is, therefore, important to have a holistic approach towards reduction of multi-layered taxes.

It is urgent for the government to implement measures such as 'green channel' for agricultural products at least along the national highways and economic corridors to speed up the movement of trucks. Measures should be taken to make check posts automatic and waiting time at the check posts should be minimum. According to respondents, a truck spends around four hours daily at various check points and tolls leading to increased travel time, fuel cost and increased chances of spoilage as a result of multiple stops and checks. Compared to this, the same product, if travelling through rail, is not stopped anywhere. To save time and fuel and prevent produce from spoilage, there is requirement to introduce green channelling for faster movement of trucks.

The respondents have further pointed out that even if GST does not happen due to lack of majority in the Upper House of the Parliament, the central government can work with the states in which it has majority such as Gujarat, Rajasthan Haryana and Maharashtra to have green channels. This will significantly benefit movement of perishable produce and reduce wastages. To implement green channel, India can learn from the EU's experiences of movement of perishable cargoes between countries and replicate it across different states.

As India is fast integrating with countries in East and South East Asia, the country needs to ensure that it has a competitive tax structure. Both direct and indirect taxes are high in India. The corporate taxes should come down to 25 per cent and the number of cess should be minimised. High corporate tax discourages foreign investors to invest in India. Subsidies should be targeted to certain sub-sectors such as pack-houses where the cost of investment may be high and profits may be low. Subsidies should be targeted towards operation of facilities and not construction of facilities. Export linked subsidies should be replaced by subsidies that are not actionable under the WTO. Further, foreign companies do not want subsides. They want a transparent tax regime, which is competitive with the ASEAN neighbours. The government should give products exported from Indian SEZs and FTWZs to the Indian domestic market the same treatment as imports from other countries.

Lack of centre-state coordination is also a crucial issue faced by foreign investors. States have a major role to play in establishing food business in India. From land allotment to crossing state-borders, businesses have to deal with the state governments at every step. Therefore state-support is extremely crucial for streamlining the food supply chain and attracting foreign investments. The decision to locate in a particular state depends on its manufacturing policy and other incentives such as infrastructural support and land acquisition, among others, offered to investors by the state government. It is important for the state governments to have conducive policies related to agricultural sourcing and remove barriers to agricultural movement and distribution which will, in turn, help them to attract investment and create employment. Farmers will also have better access to markets and get a better price for their produce. There is a need for more collaboration and synergies across polices of the central and state governments. State governments play a key role in identifying the shortages of food logistics infrastructure within their states. They can also work with UKTI and UKIBC to attract investment in areas where there are shortages.

Infrastructural support is a key input required by the food businesses in India, which can come from both centre and state. The government through right policies can support the private sector in creating world-class infrastructure such as good roads or dedicated fright corridors. Power shortage has a significant impact on the quality and shelf life of food products as they are perishable and have to be stored in certain conditions. Most facilities are dependent on electricity connected to state grid for power supply to run their operations. Inadequate power supply leads to switching over to alternate sources of fuel like diesel-run generator sets, which lead to increase in running costs. This needs to be addressed through either providing round the clock power or another form of support can be subsidisation of power and water. Further, the government can support fuel-efficient and clean technologies.

Since cold storages, warehouses, pack-houses have developed in a sporadic manner in India, the information about the existing infrastructure is scanty and it is extremely difficult to locate the availability of infrastructure online or to understand the investment gaps. While NCCD is already engaged in the exercise of drawing up an in-line portal for the same, it has been pointed out during the survey that a virtual mapping of the available infrastructure will help businesses to locate and optimally utilise the existing capacity. If the government creates an online portal through which businesses can locate infrastructure availability, businesses can plan their inventory as well as infrastructure investments by identifying the availabilities and gaps. It is also important for the government to have better data collection procedures. Different government agencies publish different data on agricultural wastages. This should not be the case.

The survey shows that there is limited knowledge about e-business portals and companies feel that there is lack of transparency in government policies. Polices have to be transparent. The customs process has to be less cumbersome and the food safety regulations, labelling conditions, etc., should be uniformly imposed across different ports of entry. The need to reduce corruptions and speed up the legal processes has been highlighted by all investors (domestic and foreign). Most importantly, as of date, the policy in India is designed in a way to favour informal players and small businesses. This encourages fragmentation of the supply chain and increases wastages. Policies should be directed towards investment in better technology, clean technology, and connecting farmers to the global markets, among others.

7.2 Sector-Specific Reforms

Some of the sector-specific reforms are as follows:

7.2 1 Storage and Warehousing

The guidelines for the storage and warehousing sector support manual warehouses and storages.

Government incentives should be directed towards scientific and automated warehouses with proper inventory management system. This will enable the warehouses to modernise. It is important to encourage more private players in this segment. Moreover, the state government can help the private sector in identifying and procuring land for warehouses and give them faster clearances, wherever required.

The warehousing sector is currently dominated by the government sector whose primary focus is procurement and not distribution. In order to develop the entire supply chain and make it competitive, the private sector needs to step in. Hence, the idea needs to change from warehouse creation to warehouse management which includes bringing in greater technology, increasing the throughputs of the warehouse. The government and the private sector can also work hand-in-hand by virtue of PPP models. Though this model has been adopted by FCI, wherein they are planning to build silos on PPP model, but larger focus is required in this area going forward. As per the Report of the High Level Committee on Reorienting the Role and Restructuring of Food Corporation of India (page 31),[2]

> Outsourcing storage and movement through Public Private Partnerships by the Food Corporation of India on a competitive bidding basis would provide the required investments and managerial competence to the industry for effectively managing the supply chain. Report also states that wherever required, government can provide existing land/facilities to the PPPs.

7.2.2 Cold-chain

In the past subsides in cold-chain sector were skewed towards development of cold storages only, which led to mushrooming of cold storages and its fragmented growth. On the other hand, there are shortages of pack-houses and refrigerated trucks. Further, the

2. Available at *http://fci.gov.in/app/webroot/upload/News/Report%20of%20the%20High%20Level%20Committee%20on%20Reorienting%20the%20Role%20and%20Restructuring%20of%20FCI_English.pdf* (accessed on 28 March 2016).

cold storages are not uniformly spread across states. Thus, the incentives in the cold-chain sector have to be linked to the need of the sector, user industry and farmers. It should be targeted to states, which lack facilities, and pack-houses at the farm level. Moreover, incentives should be linked to operation, performance and use of infrastructure as many-a-times it has been observed that the infrastructure created might not lead to optimum utilisation for reasons like private sectors charge a high rental or the infrastructure may not be located in the right place.

Reduction in energy cost and availability of continuous supply of electricity are important for a viable cold-chain business. The government can offer electricity at subsidised rates to cold-chain service providers, and also subsidise the use of renewable technologies such as solar energy for developing pack-houses and cold storages. A number of companies which are present in India have pointed out that instead of subsidy they can benefit from lower interest rates. Cost of borrowing is high and cold-chains have long gestation period.

It is also pointed out during the survey that along with transport infrastructure, there is a need to construct 'truck docking stations' in fuelling stations along the national highways and state highways. The fuelling stations can have overnight facilities for drivers to stay. Along with fuelling and charging facilities, these stations can be equipped with parking, restaurants and food courts, washing and repair area, cash withdrawal facilities and internet kiosks, among others. The facilities can be subsidised for the freight vehicles while private vehicles can be charged the market rate. This will ensure that drivers of long haul vehicles work in conducive environment. This is a common phenomenon globally but in India facilities such as clean toilets and overnight stay are not available in the fuel stations. Such facilities can be developed by the private sector.

As regards mapping the infrastructure, which has been discussed earlier, there is specifically a need to develop a cold-chain grid in the country. Since the subsidies have led to fragmentation in the industry and a lot of small players have come up especially in the cold storage sub-sector, it is difficult to get the information of the available infrastructure in the country. NCCD (2015) states that the cold-chain infrastructure sector is fragmented and multiple agencies/departments are involved and the data pertaining to existing cold-chain infrastructure was not available in most of the cases. There is need to develop a robust mechanism, especially at the state level for data collection related to the cold-chain industry in India. NCCD can then develop a consolidated database of existing cold-chain infrastructure.

7.2.3 Packaging Technology

As regards the packaging sector, survey respondents from the UK have pointed out that unless the ease of business improves and supporting infrastructure is in place, they have less incentive to invest in India. In this respect, the Indian government should scale up the supporting infrastructure and initiate policies that would help modernise the food supply chain.

Further, the government can set up a manufacturing technology upgradation fund that provides finance at reduced interest rates on a medium and long term basis to help the Indian SMEs to upgrade technology. This will incentivise companies to upgrade to more modern technology. The modern technologies can help in reducing wastage in food supply chain associated with traditional methods of food packaging.

The higher taxes on processed vis-a-vis fresh produce discourages food processing and investment in packaging sector. Lower taxes on processed food will not only encourage investment in food processing and packaging technology but lead to development of India as a manufacturing hub and create employment.

Creating level playing field for the corporate sector should not be the government policy. Barriers to imports of raw materials and packaging machineries should be reduced. Although Indian governments have several incentives for cluster development, units in these clusters do not benefit from such incentives. Benefits should be targeted to both units and cluster developers. Units in SEZs are at a disadvantage to units located in India's FTA partner countries in terms of tariffs while catering to the domestic market. This issue has to be addressed. The units in SEZs should have the best FTA tariffs or else there is no incentive for companies to establish presence in Indian SEZs.

As the Indian government is focusing on reduction of packaging waste and recycling packaging raw materials, there is scope for setting up centres of excellence dedicated to green packaging. The government can invite the UK companies to invest in such centres of excellence and provide technical assistance to domestic companies.

The packaging industry is characterised by a large number of non-corporate players and traditional methods of packaging. The government can encourage

R&D in packaging technology and incentivise innovation in areas such as nanotechnology enabled packaging. The government has already come up with the 'Start-up India' policy. It can also come up with an 'Innovate India' policy as mentioned above to encourage R&D.

In India, the packaging norms are laid down by the FSSAI. The FSSAI has to closely work with the Indian packaging industry to raise awareness about the packaging norms for food safety. The FSSAI can make the food testing standards and procedures more transparent. It should also work towards aligning food safety standards to international benchmarks.

7.2.4 Skill Development

The survey shows that there is substantial enough scope for skill development across the food supply chain. The Government of India has renewed focus on skill development and is actively seeking domestic as well as international investments and collaborative initiatives in this area.

India needs to change its approach towards vocational training. At the school level, there can be seminars and workshop to get the students familiarised with vocational courses and motivate them to join such courses. There is also need for training of trainers and on-the job training. Companies will not be willing to invest in training if they have contractual employees. The labour regulation should facilitate permanent employment. The government should provide appropriate incentives for companies to move towards corporatisation and invest in skill development. For example, the government can lower corporate tax and subsidise training to promote skill development. Emphasis should be laid on employee retention and quality job creation in government policies.

Indian government should also remove barriers to foreign investment in the entire food supply chain including retail so that foreign companies establish presence in the country and bring in their supply chain agents and manufacturers. This will continue to create the demand for skilled workforce on the one hand, and, on the other, help modernise the supply chain. Foreign training and academic institutes will like to maintain their autonomy and administrative independence. The role of the Indian government is to ensure that these institutes are given the autonomy but at the same time they are of international repute and standards so that the trainees benefit from the courses.

The Indian corporate sector can be encouraged to collaborate with skill development institutes abroad for short-term online courses in warehousing, cold-chain and packaging technology. They can sponsor their employees to some of these courses such as those run by the Supply Chain Academy, UK and the Institute of Supply Chain Management, UK. National Policy for Skill Development and Entrepreneurship, 2015 also encourages companies to spend their CSR funding towards skilling their workforce. Such initiatives can help generate demand for skill development centres and training facilities.

The existing infrastructure of skill development in India in the form of ITIs needs to be improved. The government should encourage higher private sector involvement in improving the educational as well as physical infrastructure of ITIs. This would help ITIs become a prospective collaborating partner for UK institutes and companies. Further, there is need to connect the academic institutions and universities with vocational training centre. For example, engineering college professors can take some lectures in ITIs. Further, there is need for more hand-on experiences or on-the-job experiences. The vocational training institutes can partner industry so that there is on-the-job training.

7.2.5 Research and Development

There is need to speed up the patent process, strengthen the IPR regulation and protection of patents and copyrights. While there are regulations in place, there has to be serious implementation of existing laws. The government is already encouraging innovation through the 'Start-up India' campaign and there are joint R&D programmes through international collaborations. However, the success of these will depend on an enabling environment and a sound ecosystem. This includes strong laws against infringement, incubation centres and access to funding.

In India the government has somewhat neglected the focus on R&D in food supply chain. Although there are various schemes for R&D, there is hardly any support for R&D in food supply chain logistics. R&D can lead to development of new products and processes and commercialisation of this can lead to start-ups. Businesses should be given incentives for undertaking R&D in sectors such as food processing and food supply chain and these should be made priority sectors for encouraging R&D and innovation under the "Start-up India" initiative.

Since only a few companies have scale and finance to undertake R&D, it is suggested that there should be an 'Innovate India' Scheme with Corporate tax benefits and other incentives. The time frame for corporate income tax concession for R&D investment by private sector in this scheme can be for five years. A company engaged in R&D can get income tax concessions on the amount invested in R&D for a period of five years and if this innovation is commercialised, it can be further extended to a period of another three years. This will encourage private sector to invest in R&D.

The government should encourage the academic institutes and engineering colleges to collaborate more with the private sector and encourage the private sector to invest in incubation centre in these universities and technical institutes. This can be done through appropriate tax concession and other incentives. Incentives should also be provided for research in clean technologies and cost-effective technologies. The government can promote two-three specialised SEZs for R&D in select cities like Pune, Hyderabad or Bangalore in the line of China's high technology zones.

There is need to improve the quality of education and training so that the workforce is capable of undertaking the vocational training courses and on-the-job training. It is important to design standards for personnel such as those at the shop floor of cold storages, refereed vehicle drivers, forklift operators, etc. There is need for improving and skill upgradation of food safety inspectors and quality control personnel.

7.3 What UKTI and UKIBC Can Do?

The survey shows that the presence of the UK companies in India is low and the companies have pointed out that they have limited knowledge about the market. There is need for joint road shows by UKTI and UKIBC in different cities of the UK where they can provide information to the UK businesses about the Indian market. In these road shows, some domestic (for example, Future Group) and foreign corporate (McDonald's) from India can be asked to share their experiences. These can be a two-day event. On the first day, presentations can be made by corporate and experts from India while, on the second day, there can be buyer seller meet.

UKIBC and UKTI can draw up a 'Journey Map for India' or a report on 'Invest India' for the UK companies highlighting the present policies of the central and state government, how they can dovetail the policies, which are the states with ease of doing business, what kind of licences and clearances are required and what is the process, etc. This will fill up the information gap.

UKTI and UKIBC can start work with the state government in facilitating joint skill development centres, investment in warehousing and storages, etc. These are the sectors where there is strong government presence in India.

There is need to build up more awareness in India about the strengths of the UK companies in areas such as automated storages and warehousing, FTWZs, cold storages using renewable technologies, fuel-efficient technologies in refereed vehicle, planning and layout of service stations along national highways, skill development in supply chain management and in R&D in packaging technology and other areas of food supply chain. For this there can be events across major cities in India where central and state-level policymakers, businesses and academics can participate.

There is need for more interaction with media in India and the UK. Regular articles on success stories in India can help to attract businesses and collaborations. UKIBC and UKTI can examine the possibility of engaging a public relation agency in India for media publicity of their research and potential areas of collaboration. The media publicity can also focus on removal of trade barriers. The role of the public relation agency will be to get media slots where eminent personalities can write articles on issues that will enhance India-UK trade and investment in food supply chain which will lead to benefits for both the Indian and the UK companies.

The website developed under the project (*http://www.foodlogistics.in/*) can be used to disseminate information about the Indian market to the UK companies. UKIBC has a link to this website. The website has provision for uploading new research articles and news on food supply chain in India and the UK. UKTI can also be linked to this website and key research findings can be shared through this website for wider dissemination. For this to be successful, the website has to be maintained and updated on a regular basis. A small amount of fundings (around INR 800,000 USD 12,069)[3] per year can be allocated for the same.

7.4 Intergovernmental and Business-to-Business Collaborations

The survey has found that a lot of barriers can be addressed through better understanding of

3. Converted using Oanda currency converter. Available at *http://www.oanda.com/currency/converter/* (Exchange rate: INR 1 = USD 0.01509 as on 4 April 2016).

each others' strength and markets and through collaborations. Given the saturated domestic market for food products and the growing Indian market, it is in the interest of the UK companies and their associations to push for the India-EU BTIA with India. On its part, India too should be willing to move forward with the trade agreement. The India-EU BTIA will lead to lowering of tariffs for food packaging raw materials and machinery and encourage trade flows between India and the EU member states including the UK. This would help the UK companies to establish supply chain networks through India. It will incentivise the UK food packaging companies to enter the Indian market and establish manufacturing presence. At present, companies from the EU are at a disadvantage vis-a-vis companies from countries with which India has a trade agreement. Given the saturated domestic market for food products and the growing Indian market, it is in the interest of the UK companies and their associations to push for the trade agreement with India. On its part, India should continue to implement domestic reforms especially in sectors such as multi-brand retail which will encourage food processing and packaging companies from the UK to come and invest in India. If India does not sign the trade agreement with the EU, the UK companies will export to India through the ASEAN and other trade agreements, which can lead to trade distortion and India may not become a part of the global production network of the UK and other EU companies. In spite of the several reform announcements in the recent past, India has not received a major investment in the food supply chain and, hence, it is important for the Indian government to have a relook into its policies. Unless the government does so, initiatives such as 'Make in India' will not be successful.

India and the UK are different markets in terms of their tastes, preferences, geographical conditions, infrastructure requirements, etc. As a result, it is important to customise the products to suit the requirements of the Indian market. This requires not only market research but also testing products in the Indian market and collecting robust feedback. There is a need for collaboration between the government and business councils of the two countries in order to understand the regulations, operating conditions and market requirements. Study tours and field visits to the UK will help the Indian policymakers (such as the FSSAI) understand issues such as the food safety and labelling requirements, standards of testing laboratories, etc.

The survey shows that there is scope for joint R&D programme.[4] For joint R&D programmes between India and the UK in food supply chain, joint funds should be made available and common criteria should be laid down for evaluation of the joint R&D after discussions with stakeholders from both the countries. Further, wherever government funding is not feasible, private players, angel investors and venture capitalists should be identified. Since the Indian government has already started the 'Start-up India' initiative, the UK can be a key partner in this initiative. UKIBC and UKTI can share information about this initiative among their members. Information sharing and support can be given for collaborative start-ups between India and the UK SMEs through business-to-business meetings, seminars and workshop. Further, in the India-EU BTIA there can be a chapter on R&D collaborations. India and the EU can identify food logistics and supply chain as one of the key areas for such collaborations and cooperation.

The survey also shows that there are possibilities of establishing a joint skill development centre in food supply chain.[5] The Indian and the UK governments should work towards facilitating initiatives in skill development in the food supply chain logistics as part of their joint business collaboration. Food supply chain sector in India and the UK differ in terms of technological capabilities. Thus, skill development courses and training programmes offered in the UK have to be carefully customised according to the requirements of the Indian industry. For this purpose, the UK institutes and organisations have to work closely with their Indian counterparts and the industry in India to design appropriate curriculum for skill training. Organisations such as UKTI, UKIBC and the UK India Skills Forum should facilitate private investments and participation in the area of skill development by the UK institutes and academic institutions. Further, the on-going India-EU BTIA negotiations should focus on the area of investment in food supply chain logistics and there should be a separate chapter on cooperation in skill development in the agreement. This chapter can identify some areas for joint skill development.

---

4. For details on joint R&D programmes see *http://foodlogistics.in/wp-content/uploads/2016/03/Potential_for_Developing_a_Joint_Research_and_Development_Centre.pdf.pdf* (accessed on 4 April 2016).
5. Details of the centre are available at *http://foodlogistics.in/wp-content/uploads/2016/03/Concept_Plan_cum_Feasibility_Assessment_Skill_Development.pdf* (accessed on 4 April 2016).

The survey shows that there is scope for attracting investment from the UK in the development a cold-chain network and cold-chain grid.[6] The Indian and the UK governments should try to attract investments from the UK in FTWZs, agri-zones, SEZs and in establishing warehouses and storage facilities along economic corridors and ports. While the UK government and business councils can help identify the potential investors, Indian government can provide easier clearances, access to land and other infrastructure. UKTI and UKIBC can work with the Indian state governments to identify one or two clusters within the state where the UK companies can locate in India. Precisely, they can select food parks such as mega food parks or plastic clusters.

There are several barriers to movement of people, and the UK work permit and visa regime has been referred to as restrictive by survey participants. Both countries should ease movement of people, especially skilled workforce, trainees, trainers and professionals. Short-term business visitors should have visa-on-arrival in the UK. The Indian and the UK governments should work towards lowering the visa costs and the visa application processing time to facilitate frequent movement of trainees, trainers and skilled personnel. The visa regime should facilitate twinning programmes. There should be possibilities for Indian trainees to work in the UK for short duration such as 1-2 months. If Indians trained in the UK are allowed to work for a short duration, it will help them to partly compensate for the high cost of training. The UK will also gain as Indians are keen to take up education and training in the UK and are willing to pay for the same. The two countries can then take forward the twinning programme and joint training programmes.

There is need for collaboration and sharing of knowledge among the packaging institutes of the two countries. The key component of the knowledge sharing would involve use of the right raw materials, proper handling procedures, etc. UKIBC and its member companies can collaborate with associations such as Indian Institute of Packaging to offer training and curricula designing for training in modern packaging technologies to the Indian companies. UKIBC and its member companies can also participate in packaging exhibitions such as PackPlus, an annual packaging, processing and supply chain event organised by the Indian Institute of Packaging. This will offer the UK companies a platform to exhibit new technologies and interact with prospective Indian collaborators.

The industry associations of the two countries play an important role in facilitating collaborations between the Indian and the UK companies. Organisations such as UKIBC and UKTI can help the UK companies identify the right partner in India and support feasibility studies of the Indian packaging industry. UKIBC can do a study on 'how to set up a manufacturing facility in India' highlighting the procedures and regulations. Smaller UK companies are not able to fund for individual feasibility studies and they would benefit if UKIBC or UKTI provide them the information. They also need information in other areas such as the food safety and standards, labelling requirements, availability of raw materials, sourcing networks and value chain, liberalisation of the packaging sector under India's different trade agreement and compliance standards for packaging companies in India, among others.

If the above reforms are implemented, it will help strengthen the Indian food supply chain through collaborations with the UK. All players in the supply chain from farmers to consumers will benefit from greater investment and reduction in wastages.

6. For details on the Cold-chain Grid Map see *http://foodlogistics.in/wp-content/uploads/2016/02/Cold_Chain-_Grid_in_India.pdf* (accessed on 4 April 2016).

References

Aranca (2012). *Packaging Industry: A Review*. Report Prepared for ASSOCHAM Packaging Summit 2012. Mumbai. Available at *http://www.aranca.com/downloads/special-reports/The-Aranca-Report-Packaging-Industry-A-Review.pdf* (accessed 11 March 2016).

Baker, P. (2007). "An Explanatory Framework of the Role of Inventory and Warehousing in International Supply Chains", *International Journal of Logistics Management* 18(1): 64-80. Available at *https://core.ac.uk/download/files/23/138561.pdf* (accessed on 26 March 2016).

Battelle (2013). *2014 Global R&D Funding Forecast*. December. Available at *http://www.battelle.org/docs/tpp/2014_global_rd_funding_forecast.pdf* (accessed on 18 September 2015).

Centre for Market Research & Social Development (CMSD) (2013). *Technology Gap Assessment in Packaging Techniques in MSME Sector*. New Delhi: CMSD Pvt. Ltd.

Chari, Anusha and T.C.A. Madhav Raghavan (2012). "Foreign Direct Investment in India's Retail Bazaar: Opportunities and Challenges", *The World Economy* 35(1): 79-90.

Christopher, M., H. Peck and D. Towill (2006). "A Taxonomy for Selecting Global Supply Chain Strategies", *International Journal of Logistics Management* 17(2): 277-87.

Coles, R. and M.J. Kirwan (2011). *Food and Beverage Packaging Technology*. John Wiley & Sons.

Cornell University, INSEAD and WIPO (2015). *The Global Innovation Index 2015: Effective Innovation Policies for Development*. Ithaca and Geneva: Fontainebleau. Available at *https://www.globalinnovationindex.org/content/page/gii-full-report-2015/#pdfopener* (accessed on 18 September 2015).

Ernst & Young (E&Y) (2012). *Knowledge Paper on Skill Development in India: Learner First*. Ernst & Young Private Limited. Available at *http://www.ey.com/Publication/vwLUAssets/FICCI_skill_report_2012_finalversion/$FILE/FICCI_skill_report_2012_finalversion_low_resolution.pdf* (accessed on 8 October 2015).

———. (2013). *Unwrapping the Packaging Industry: Seven Factors for Success*. EYGM Limited. Available at *http://www.ey.com/Publication/vwLUAssets/Unwrapping_the_packaging_industry_%E2%80%93_seven_factors_for_success/$FILE/EY_Unwrapping_the_packaging_industry_-_seven_success_factors.pdf* (Accessed 11 March 2016).

Ernst & Young and Confederation of Indian Industries (CII) (2013). *The Indian Warehousing Industry: An Overview*. India: Ernst & Young and CII. October. Available at *http://www.ey.com/Publication/vwLUAssets/The-Indian-Warehousing-Industry-An-Overview/$FILE/EY-The-Indian-Warehousing-Industry-An-Overview.pdf* (accessed on 26 March 2016).

Fernie, J and Leigh Sparks (2004). *Logistics and Retail Management: Insights into Current Practice and Trends from Leading Experts*. United Kingdom: Kogan Page Limited.

FICCI (2014). *Potential of Plastics Industry in Northern India with Special Focus on Plasticulture and Food Processing: A Report on Plastics Industry*. New Delhi: Federation of Indian Chambers of Commerce and Industry.

Hilletofth, P. (2009). "How to Develop a Differentiated Supply Chain Strategy", *Industrial Management & Data Systems* 109(1): 16-33.

Images Multimedia Private Limited (2015). *India Retail Report: 2015*. New Delhi: Images Group.

Indian Brand Equity Foundation (IBEF) (2013). *Indian Logistics Industry: Gaining Momentum: A Report on the Performance and Emerging Trends in the Indian Logistics Industry*. November. Available at *http://www.ibef.org/download/indian-logistics-industry-gaining-momentum.pdf* (accessed on 22 September 2015).

Infrastructure Development Finance Company (2012). *Skill Development in India: A Transformation in the Making*. December. Available at: *http://www.idfc.com/pdf/report/2012/Chapter_18.pdf* (accessed on 3 March 2016).

International Netherlands Group (ING) and Institute of Transport and Maritime Management Antwerp (ITMMA) (2012). *Economic Analysis of the Warehousing and Distribution Market in Northwest Europe*. Presentation at the Press Meeting in Brussels on 25 September. Available at *http://www.ing.be/xpedio/groups/internet/@public/@bbl/@secr_gen_et_comm/@revue_presse/documents/portalcontent/553532_en.pdf* (accessed on 26 March 2016).

International Association of Refrigerated Warehouses (IARW) (2010). *Global Cold Storage Capacity Report*. Prepared by Victoria Salin, Texas A&M University for the IARW, Virginia. Available at *http://www.gcca.org/wp-content/uploads/2012/10/2010_Capacity_Report.pdf* (accessed on 27 March 2016).

International Labour Organization (ILO) (2012). *International Standard Classification of Occupations: Structure, Group Definitions and Correspondence Tables*. Geneva. Available at *http://www.ilo.org/wcmsp5/groups/public/---dgreports/---dcomm/---publ/documents/publication/wcms_172572.pdf* (accessed on 1 October 2015).

Knight Frank (2014). *India Logistics & Warehousing Report*. India. Available at: *http://content.knightfrank.com/research/677/documents/en/india-warehousing-and-logistics-report-2326.pdf* (accessed on 3 October 2015).

Koskinen, P. and O.P. Hilmola (2008). "Supply Chain Challenges of North European Paper Industry", *Industrial Management & Data Systems* 108(2): 208-27.

KPMG (2007). *Skill Gaps in the Indian Logistics Sector: A White Paper*. Available at *http://www.in.kpmg.com/pdf/logistics.pdf* (accessed on 1 October 2015).

Kushwaha D.W. and T. Nath (2015). "Skill Gaps Analysis in Food Processing Industry with Special Reference to Fruits and Vegetables", *Asian Journal of Science and Applied Technology* 4(2): 31-40. Available at *http://www.trp.org.in/wp-content/uploads/2015/12/AJSAT-Vol.4-No.2-July-December-2015-pp.31-40.pdf* (accessed on 28 March 2016).

Lama, S. (2012). "Vocational Education and Training: The Role of ODL", *International Journal of Scientific and Research Publications* 2(3), March. Available at *http://www.ijsrp.org/research_paper_mar2012/ijsrp-Mar-2012-30.pdf* (accessed 9 October 2015).

Lucintel (2012). *Global Warehousing and Storage Industry 2012-2017: Trend, Profit and Forecast Analysis*. November. Available at: *http://www.lucintel.com/reports/mass_transportation/global_warehousing_and_storage_industry_2012_2017_trend_profit_and_forecast_analysis_november_2012.aspx* (accessed on 26 March 2016).

Ministry of Agriculture (2008). *The Report of the Task Force on Development of Cold Chain in India*. New Delhi: Department of Agriculture and Cooperation, Government of India.

Ministry of Finance (2015). *Economic Survey 2014-15*. Chapter 9. New Delhi. Available at *http://www.indiabudget.nic.in/es2014-15/echapvol2-09.pdf* (accessed on 1 October 2015).

Ministry of Food Processing Industries (MoFPI) and Yes Bank (2014). *Fruits & Vegetables Availability Maps of India*. New Delhi. Available at *http://mofpi.nic.in/H_Dwld.aspx?KYEwmOL+HGqTV0f1VSVZLW3VlDC+YHsvTxu0wQ5UZV5yHmWs6HjdrQ==* (accessed on 28 March 2016).

Ministry of Labour and Employment (2014). *Report on Employment-Unemployment Survey 1, 2013-14*. Chandigarh: Government of India.

Ministry of Skill Development and Entrepreneurship (2015). *National Policy on Skill Development and Entrepreneurship*. New Delhi. Available at *http://www.msde.gov.in/assets/images/Skill%20India/policy%20booklet-%20Final.pdf* (accessed on 1 October 2015).

Mukherjee, A., T.M. Goyal, P. Pal and S. Deb (2014). *Food Supply Chain in India: Analysing the Potential for International Business*. New Delhi: Academic Foundation.

National Centre for Cold-chain Development (NCCD) (2015). *All India Cold-chain Infrastructure Capacity: Assessment of Status & Gap*. NCCD and NABCON. Available at *http://www.nccd.gov.in/PDF/CCSG_Final%20Report_Web.pdf* (accessed on 9 December 2015).

————. (2014). *Report of the Task Force on Cold Chain Projects*. Prepared for the MoFPI by NCCD, Government of India, New Delhi, India. Available at *http://www.nccd.gov.in/PDF/Final-ReportTFCP.pdf* (accessed on 26 March 2016).

National Sample Survey Office (NSSO) (2013). *Status of Education and Vocational Training in India*. March. New Delhi: NSSO, Ministry of Statistics and Programme Implementation, Government of India.

National Skill Development Corporation (NSDC) (2009). *Human Resource and Skill Requirement in the Transportation, Logistics, Warehousing and Packaging Sector (2022)*. Available at *http://www.nsdcindia.org/sites/default/files/files/transportation-logistics-2009.pdf* (accessed on 1 October 2009).

NSDC and KPMG (2014). *Human Resource and Skill Requirements in the Transportation, Logistics, Warehousing & Packaging Sector (2013-17, 2017-22)*. Prepared by KPMG for NSDC, New Delhi. Available at *http://www.safeducate.com/PDF/KPMG%20Report%20on%20Logistics,%20Transportation%20and%20Warehousing%20(2013-2017,%202017-2022).pdf* (accessed on 8 October 2015).

Parfitt, J., M. Barthel and S. Macnaughton (2010). "Food Waste within Food Supply Chains: Quantification and Potential for Change to 2050", *Philosophical Transaction of the Royal Society Biological Sciences* 365(1554): 3065-81. Available at *http://rstb.royalsocietypublishing.org/content/365/1554/3065* (accessed on 28 March 2016).

Planning Commission (2012). *The Committee on Encouraging Investments in Supply Chains Including Provision for Cold Storages for More Efficient Distribution of Farm Produce*. New Delhi: Development Policy Division, Government of India. Available at: *http://planningcommission.gov.in/reports/genrep/rep_supply1312.pdf* (accessed on 28 March 2016).

PricewaterhouseCoopers (PwC) (2012). *Next-generation Supply Chains: Efficient, Fast and Tailored: Global Supply Chain Survey 2013*. United Kingdom: Pricewaterhouse Coopers LLP. Available at *http://www.pwc.be/en/supply-chain-management/assets/global_supply_chain_survey_2013.pdf* (accessed on 1 October 2015).

————. (2011). *Building Warehousing Competitiveness*. July. India. Available at *https://www.pwc.in/assets/pdfs/publications-2011/building-warehousing-competitiveness-india.pdf* (accessed on 26 March 2016)

Robertson, G.L. (2012). *Food Packaging: Principles and Practice*. CRC Press.

Smith, David and Leigh Sparks (2004). "Temperature Controlled Supply Chain", in J. Fernie and Leigh Sparks (eds.), *Logistics and Retail Management: Insights into Current Practice and Trends from Leading Experts*. United Kingdom: Kogan Page Limited.

Smithers Pira (2013). *The Future of Global Packaging to 2018*. USA. Available at *http://www.smitherspira.com/news/2013/december/global-packaging-industry-market-growth-to-2018* (accessed 10 June 2015).

TeamLease and Indian Institute of Job Training (IIJT) (2009). *India Labour Report 2009: The Geographic Mismatch & A Ranking of Indian States by their Labour Ecosystem*. A Report by TeamLease and IIJT. Available at *http://www.teamlease.com/media/1149/teamlease_labourreport2009.pdf* (accessed on 22 September 2015).

Warehouse Development and Regulatory Authority (WRDA) (2014). *Annual Report 2013-14*. New Delhi, India: Government of India. Available at: *http://wdra.nic.in/Annual%20Report%20(english)%202013-2014.pdf* (accessed on 26 March 2016)